Spell it out

If it's worth saying, say it with cross stitch!

These 21 all-new alphabets set the mood for stitching any thought you'd like to convey. They're perfect for framing or for embellishing your sewing projects. As an added convenience, designer Joan Elliott included the uppercase and lowercase alphabets to match. Cross stitchers know they can rely on Joan for lovingly detailed designs, because she has brightened their worlds with her creative imaginings for over thirty years. Why not let Joan's alphabets inspire you to stitch whimsical pirates and teddy bears, or elegant creations like art nouveau and redwork stylings? They're excellent for gifts and décor with a personal touch!

LEISURE ARTS, INC.
Little Rock, Arkansas

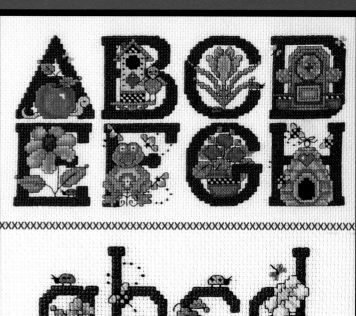

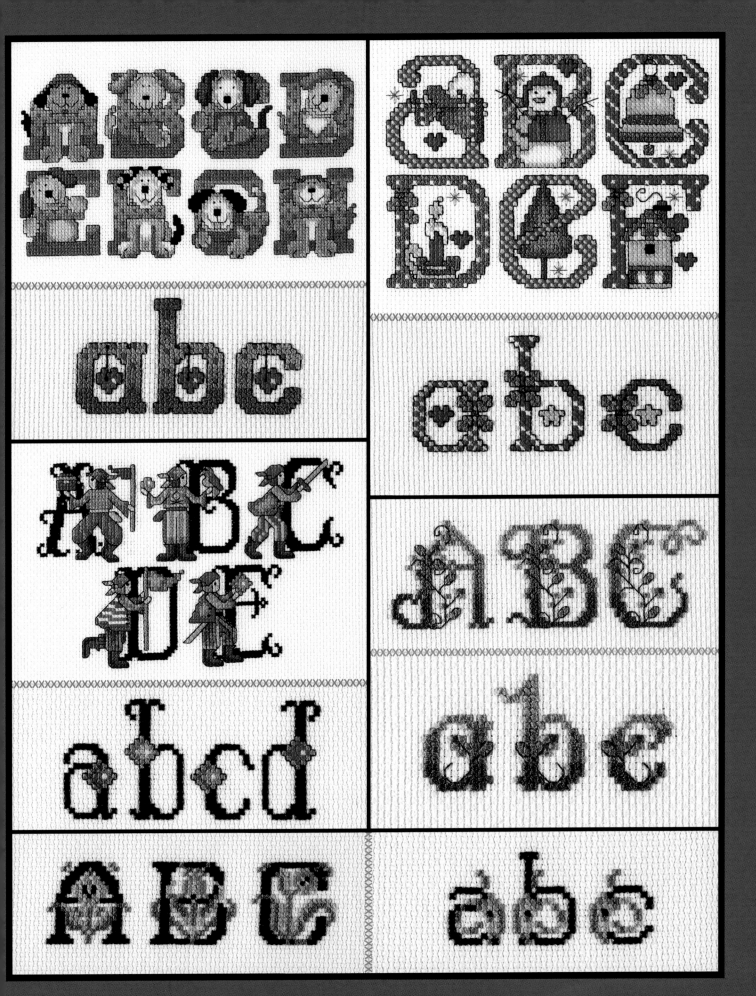

REDWORK

X	DMC	B'ST	ANC.	COLOR
♥	817		13	red
●	817		13	red Fr. Knot

Center desired letter in the decorative
border charted here around the letter A.

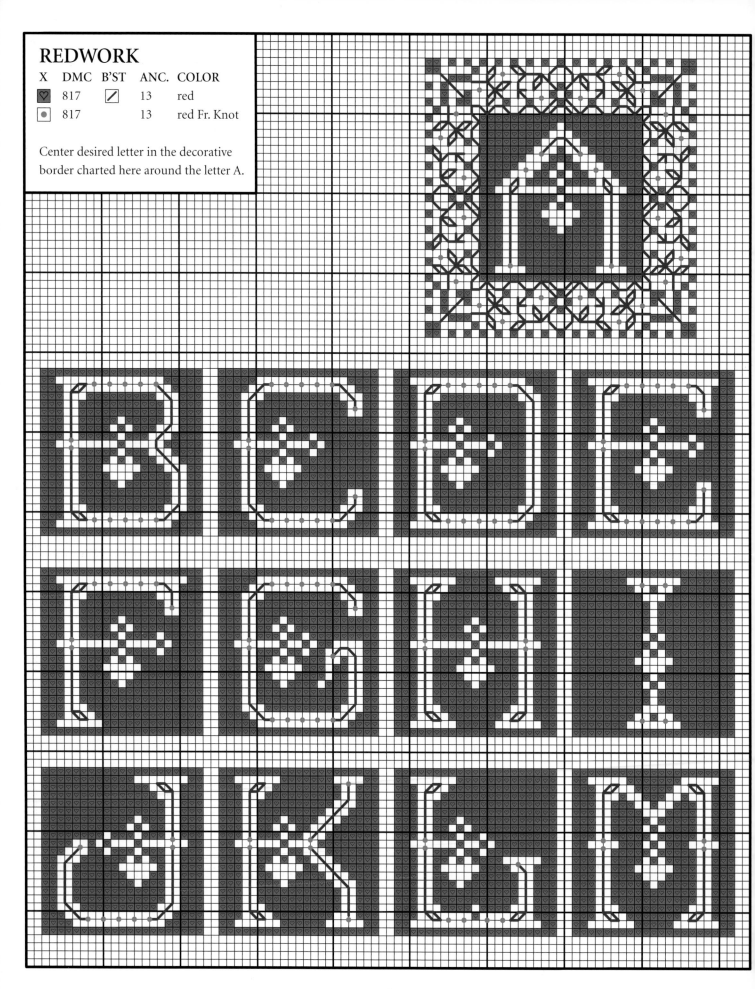

4

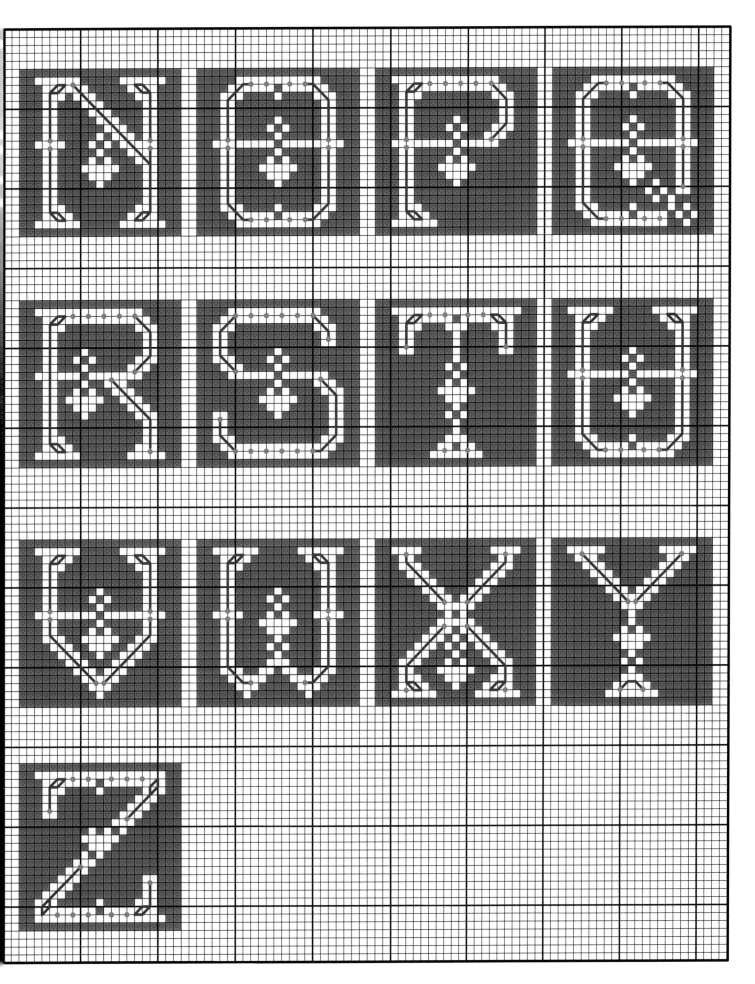

GARDENER'S ALPHABET

X	DMC	¼X	B'ST	ANC.	COLOR
☆	blanc			2	white
▲	208			110	dk lavender
◙	209			109	lavender
♡	210			108	lt lavender
■	310			403	black
◆	312			979	dk blue
✚	334			977	blue
✛	350			11	red
7	351			10	lt red
V	415			398	grey
9	434			310	brown
5	435			1046	lt brown
✿	602			63	dk pink
H	603			62	pink
8	605			1094	lt pink
m	676			891	lt gold

X	DMC	¼X	B'ST	ANC.	COLOR
4	729			890	gold
c	741			304	orange
★	742			303	dk yellow
)	743			302	yellow
−	744			301	lt yellow
♠	801			359	dk brown
♥	817			13	dk red
✳	906			256	green
Ⅲ	907			255	lt green
○	945			881	peach
◇	986			246	dk green
#	3755			140	lt blue
2	3811			1060	turquoise
◆◆	3829			901	dk gold
●	310			403	black Fr. Knot
●	743			302	yellow Fr. Knot

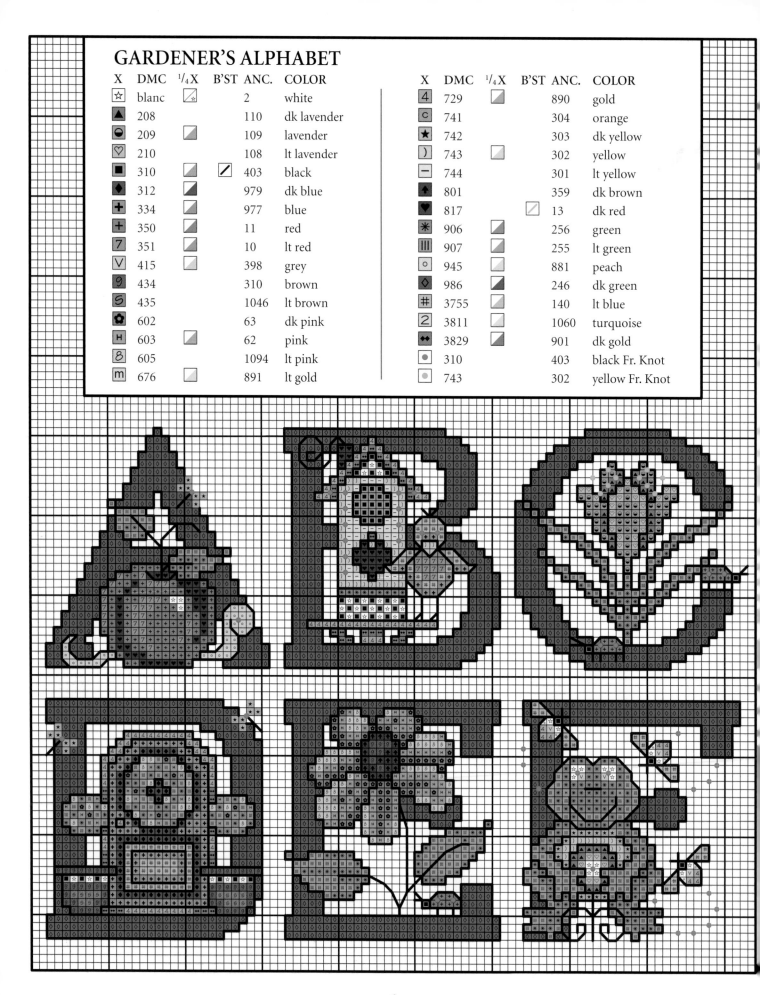

6

GARDENER'S ALPHABET

X	DMC	1/4X	B'ST	ANC.	COLOR
☆	blanc	☆		2	white
▲	208			110	dk lavender
◖	209	◪		109	lavender
♡	210			108	lt lavender
■	310	◪	◢	403	black
◆	312			979	dk blue
✛	334			977	blue
✚	350	◪		11	red
7	351			10	lt red
V	415			398	grey
9	434			310	brown
S	435			1046	lt brown
✿	602			63	dk pink
H	603			62	pink
8	605			1094	lt pink
m	676			891	lt gold

X	DMC	1/4X	ANC.	COLOR
4	729		890	gold
C	741		304	orange
★	742	◪	303	dk yellow
)	743	◪	302	yellow
—	744		301	lt yellow
♠	801		359	dk brown
♥	817		13	dk red
✳	906	◪	256	green
III	907		255	lt green
○	945	◪	881	peach
◇	986	◪	246	dk green
#	3755		140	lt blue
2	3811	◪	1060	turquoise
✦	3829	◪	901	dk gold
●	310		403	black Fr. Knot

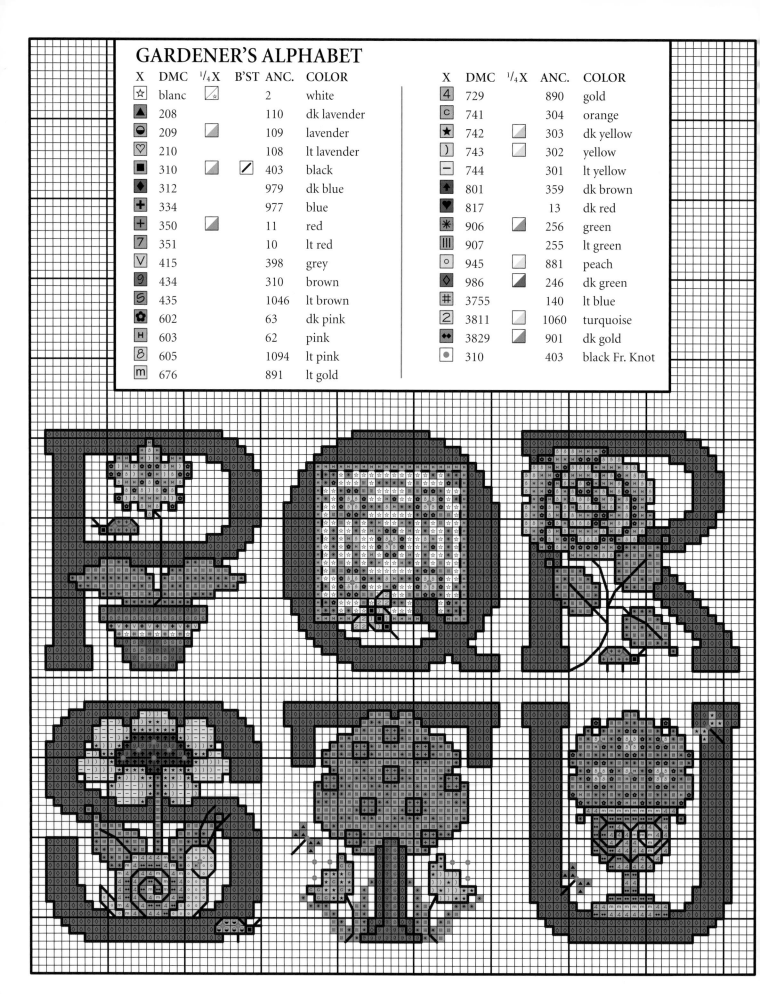

8

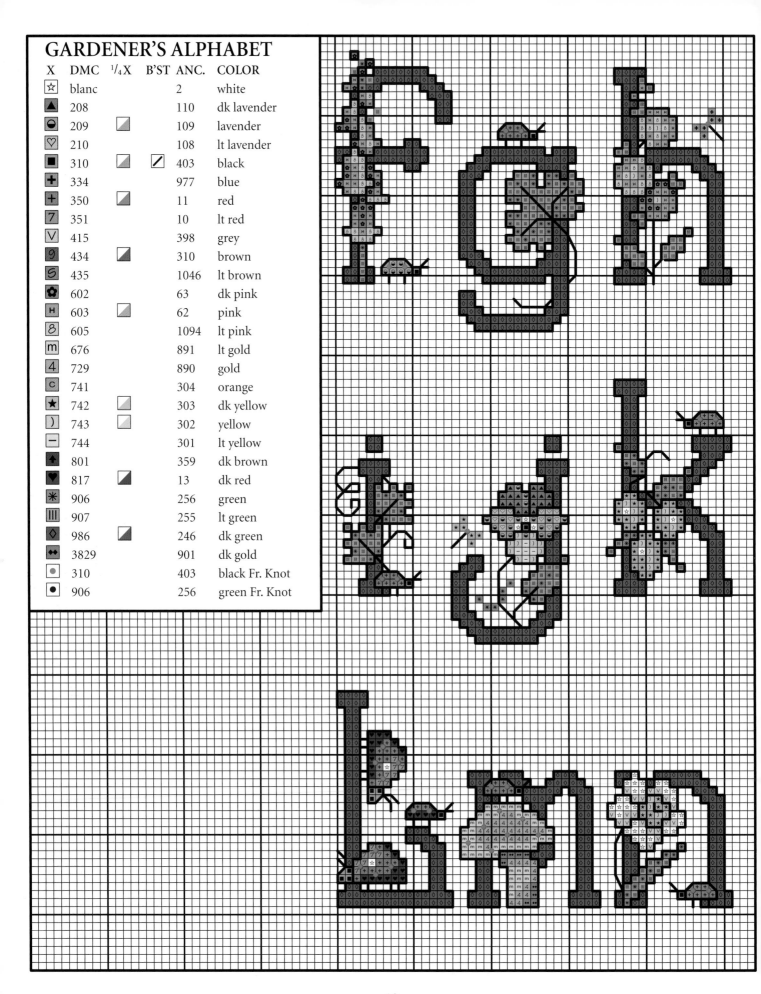

GARDENER'S ALPHABET

X	DMC	¼X	B'ST	ANC.	COLOR
☆	blanc			2	white
▲	208			110	dk lavender
◖	209	◩		109	lavender
♡	210			108	lt lavender
■	310	◩	◿	403	black
✚	334			977	blue
✚	350	◩		11	red
7	351			10	lt red
V	415			398	grey
9	434	◩		310	brown
5	435			1046	lt brown
✿	602			63	dk pink
н	603	◩		62	pink
8	605			1094	lt pink
m	676			891	lt gold
4	729			890	gold
c	741			304	orange
★	742	◩		303	dk yellow
)	743	◩		302	yellow
−	744			301	lt yellow
♠	801			359	dk brown
♥	817	◩		13	dk red
✳	906			256	green
⦀	907			255	lt green
◇	986	◩		246	dk green
✦	3829			901	dk gold
•	310			403	black Fr. Knot
●	906			256	green Fr. Knot

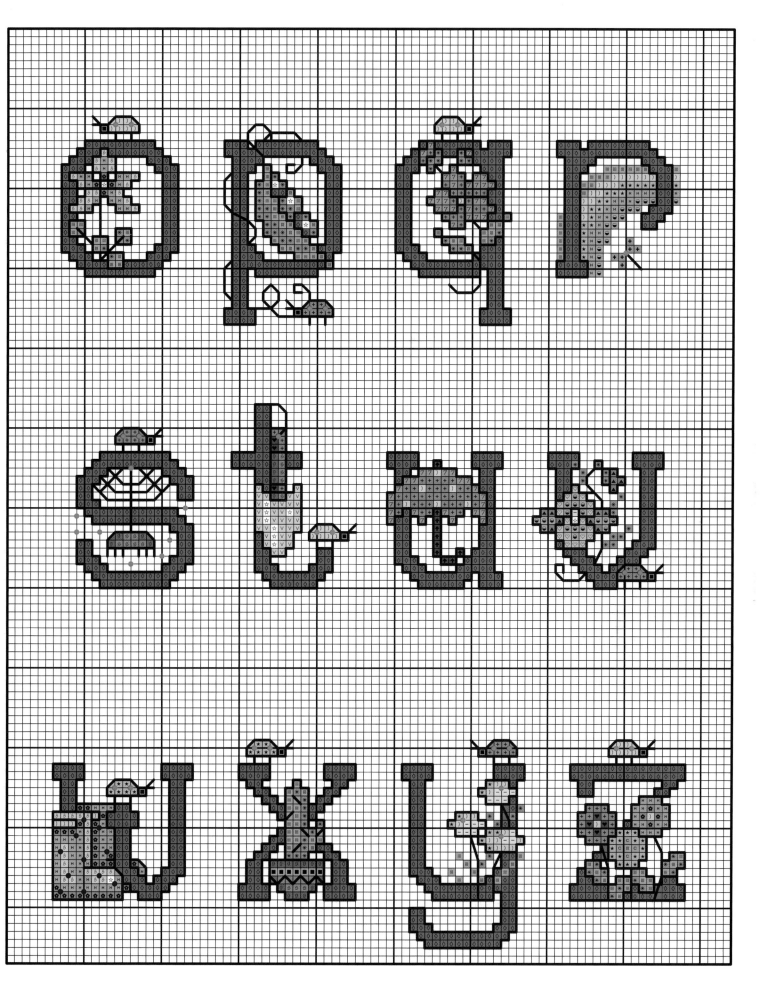

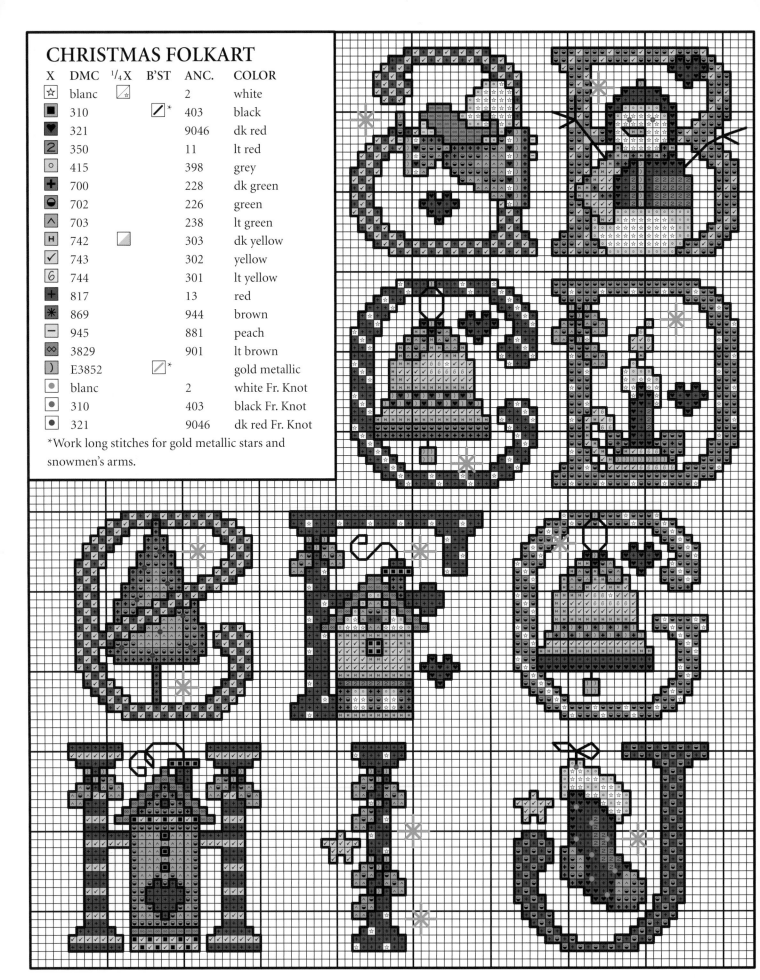

CHRISTMAS FOLKART

X	DMC	¼X	B'ST	ANC.	COLOR
☆	blanc			2	white
■	310		╱*	403	black
♥	321			9046	dk red
2	350			11	lt red
○	415			398	grey
✚	700			228	dk green
◖	702			226	green
∧	703			238	lt green
H	742	◿		303	dk yellow
✓	743			302	yellow
6	744			301	lt yellow
✛	817			13	red
✳	869			944	brown
−	945			881	peach
⊠	3829			901	lt brown
)	E3852		╱*		gold metallic
•	blanc			2	white Fr. Knot
•	310			403	black Fr. Knot
•	321			9046	dk red Fr. Knot

*Work long stitches for gold metallic stars and snowmen's arms.

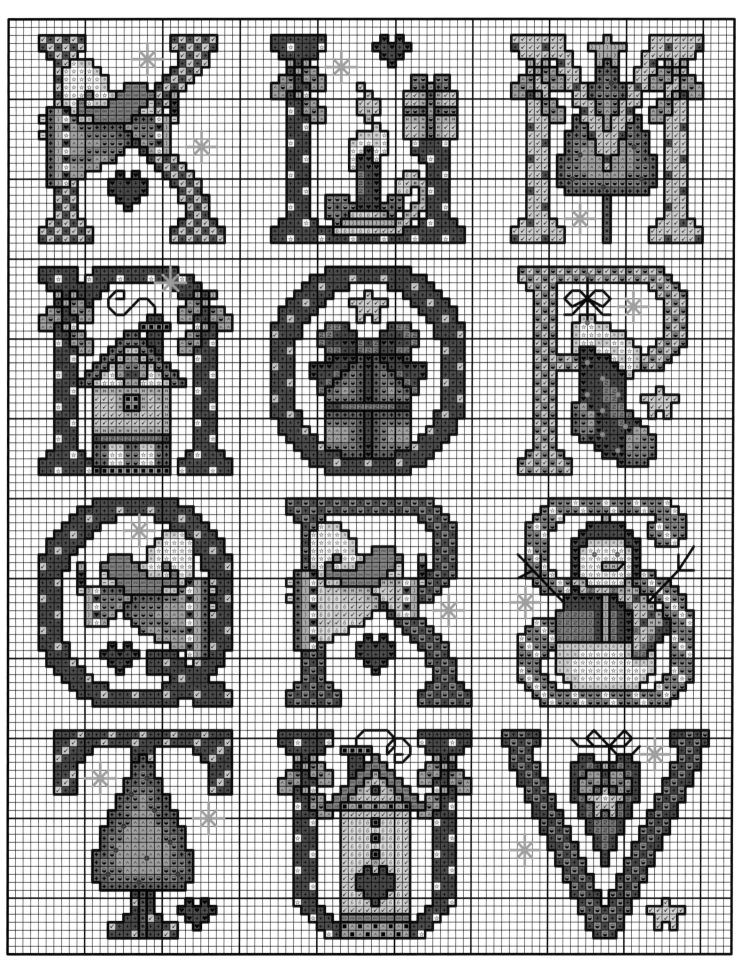

CHRISTMAS FOLKART

X	DMC	B'ST	ANC.	COLOR
☆	blanc		2	white
	310	╱	403	black
♥	321		9046	dk red
2	350		11	lt red
○	415		398	grey
✚	700		228	dk green
⊖	702		226	green
∧	703		238	lt green
H	742		303	dk yellow
✓	743		302	yellow
6	744		301	lt yellow
✛	817		13	red
)	E3852	╱ *		gold metallic
●	blanc		2	white Fr. Knot
●	310		403	black Fr. Knot

*Work long stitches for gold metallic stars.

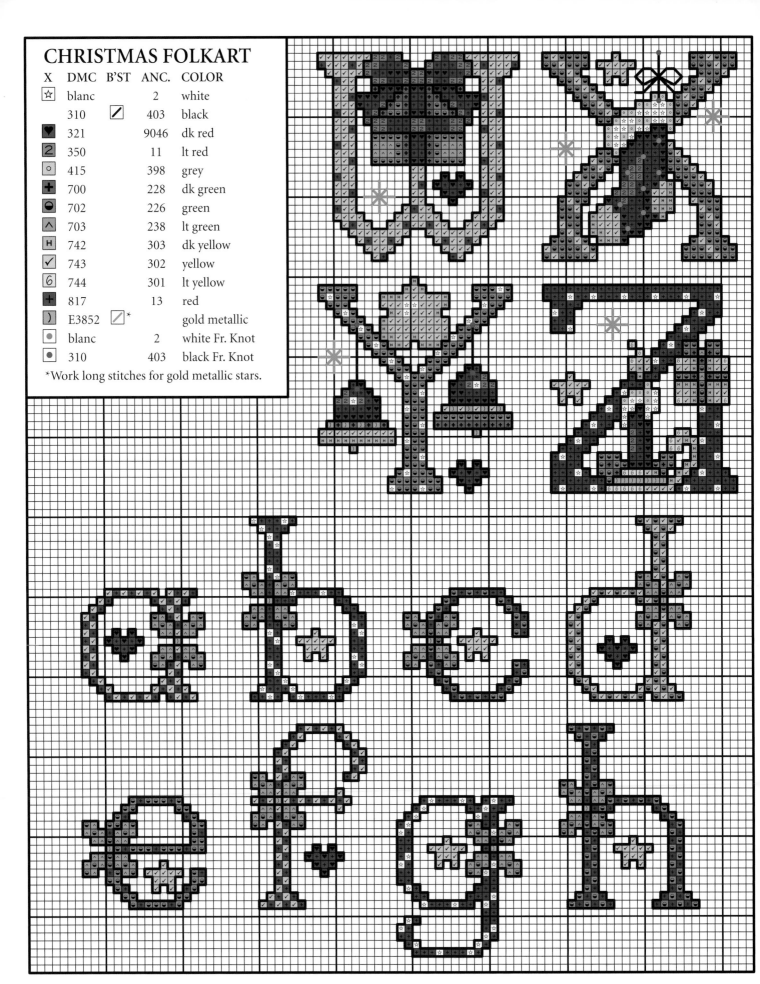

14

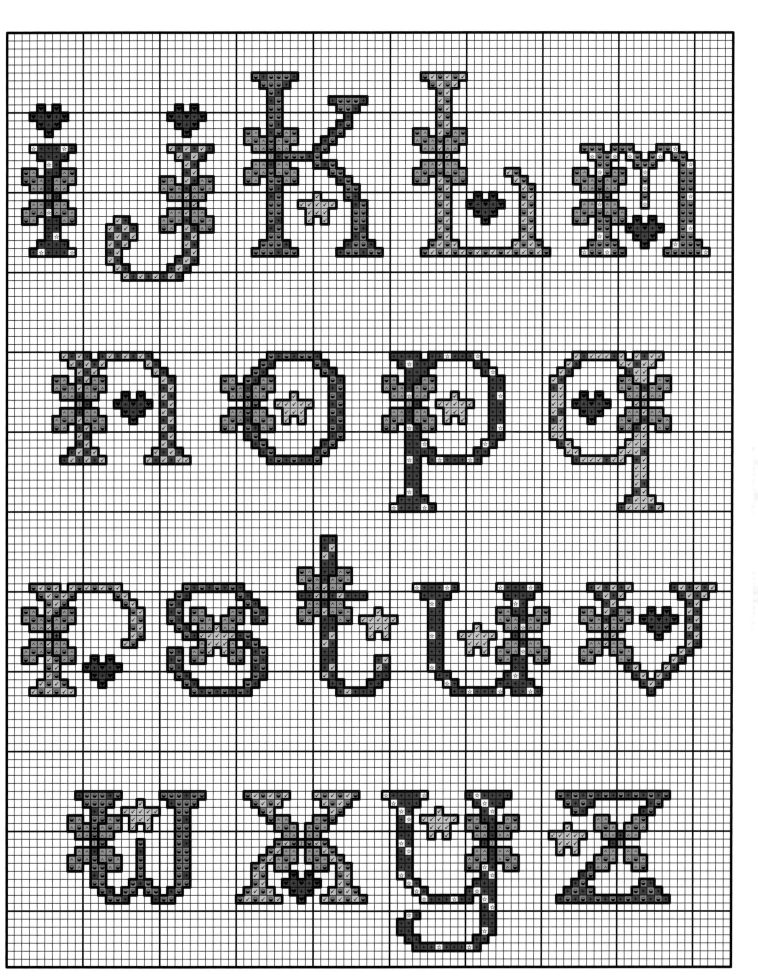

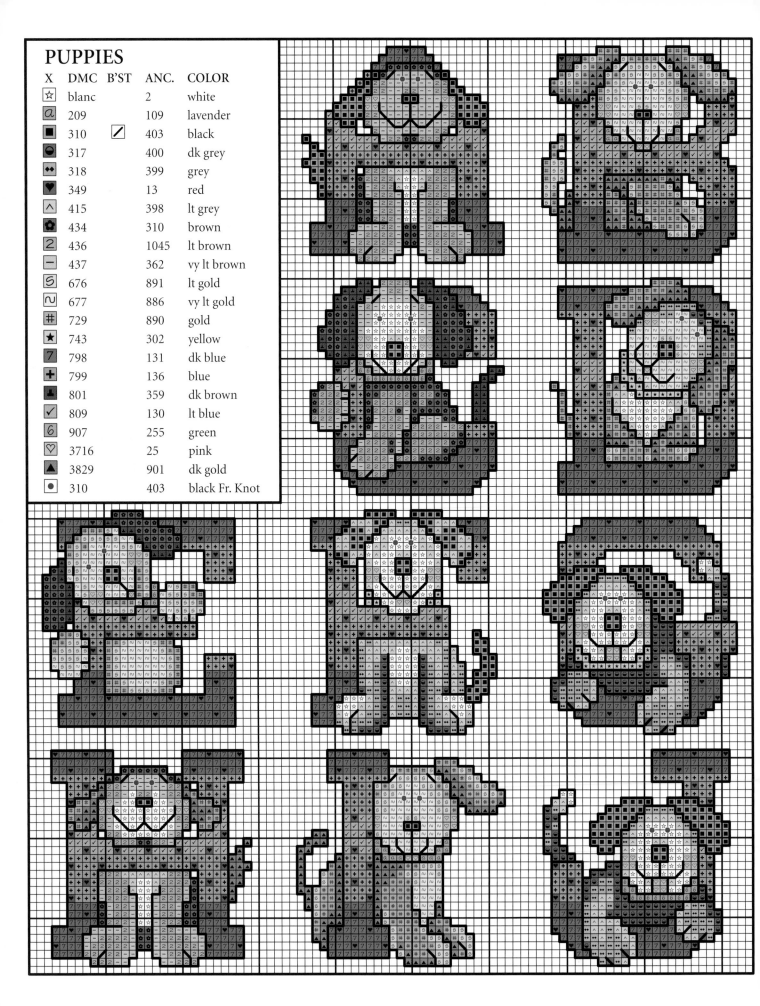

PUPPIES

X	DMC	B'ST	ANC.	COLOR
☆	blanc		2	white
ⓐ	209		109	lavender
■	310	╱	403	black
◖	317		400	dk grey
✦✦	318		399	grey
♥	349		13	red
∧	415		398	lt grey
✿	434		310	brown
2	436		1045	lt brown
−	437		362	vy lt brown
5	676		891	lt gold
∿	677		886	vy lt gold
#	729		890	gold
★	743		302	yellow
7	798		131	dk blue
✛	799		136	blue
♣	801		359	dk brown
✓	809		130	lt blue
6	907		255	green
♡	3716		25	pink
▲	3829		901	dk gold
●	310		403	black Fr. Knot

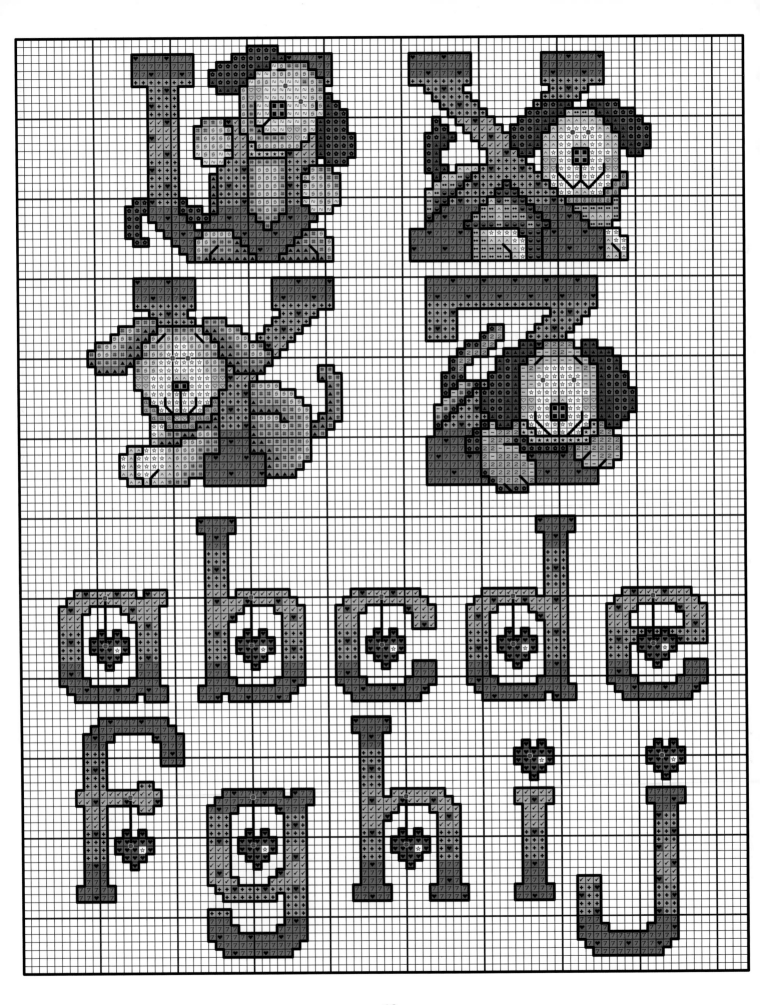

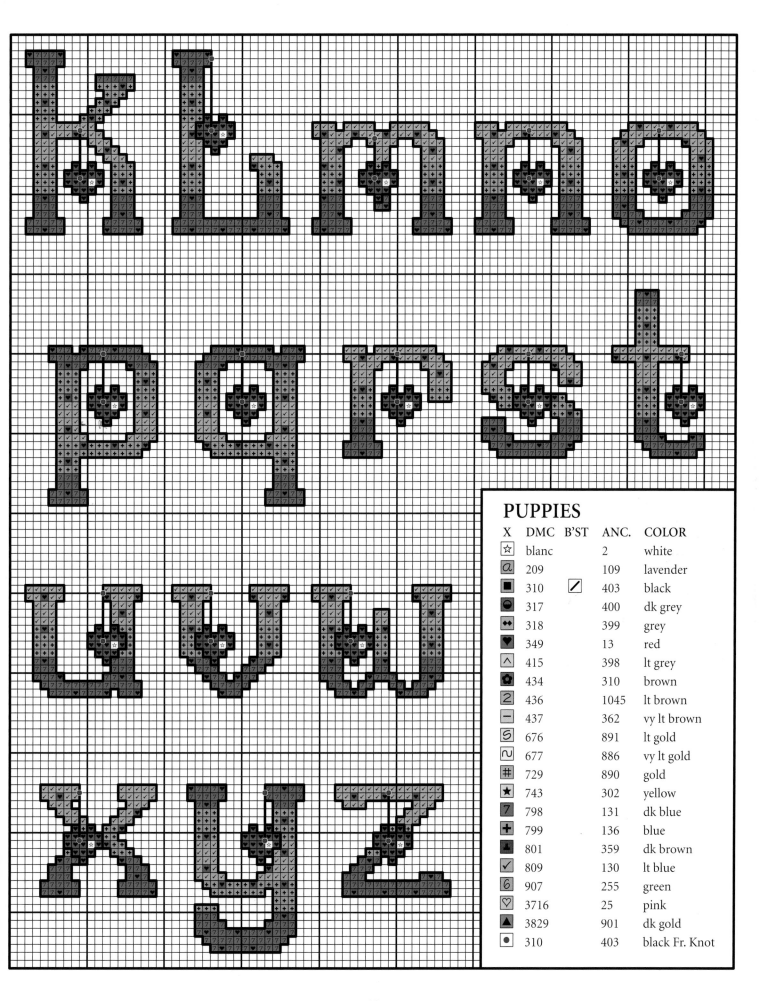

PUPPIES

X	DMC	B'ST	ANC.	COLOR
☆	blanc		2	white
a	209		109	lavender
■	310	/	403	black
◐	317		400	dk grey
◆◆	318		399	grey
♥	349		13	red
∧	415		398	lt grey
✿	434		310	brown
2	436		1045	lt brown
−	437		362	vy lt brown
S	676		891	lt gold
N	677		886	vy lt gold
#	729		890	gold
★	743		302	yellow
7	798		131	dk blue
+	799		136	blue
▲	801		359	dk brown
✓	809		130	lt blue
6	907		255	green
♡	3716		25	pink
▲	3829		901	dk gold
●	310		403	black Fr. Knot

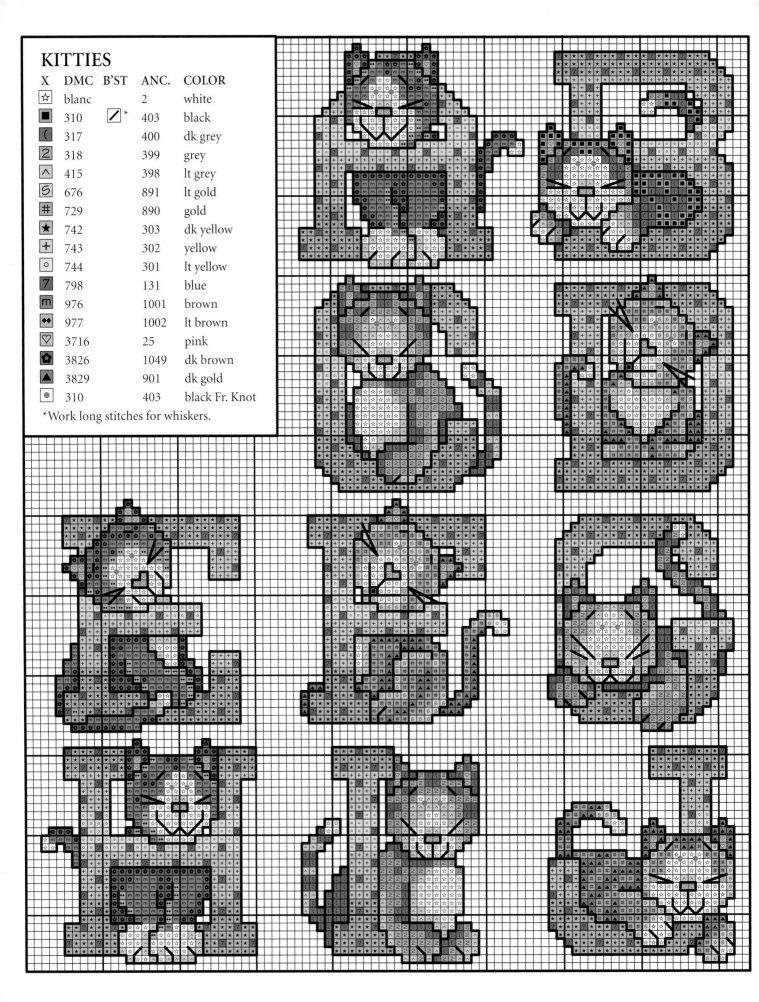

KITTIES

X	DMC	B'ST	ANC.	COLOR
☆	blanc		2	white
■	310	╱ *	403	black
⟨	317		400	dk grey
2	318		399	grey
∧	415		398	lt grey
S	676		891	lt gold
#	729		890	gold
★	742		303	dk yellow
+	743		302	yellow
○	744		301	lt yellow
7	798		131	blue
m	976		1001	brown
◆◆	977		1002	lt brown
♡	3716		25	pink
✿	3826		1049	dk brown
▲	3829		901	dk gold
•	310		403	black Fr. Knot

*Work long stitches for whiskers.

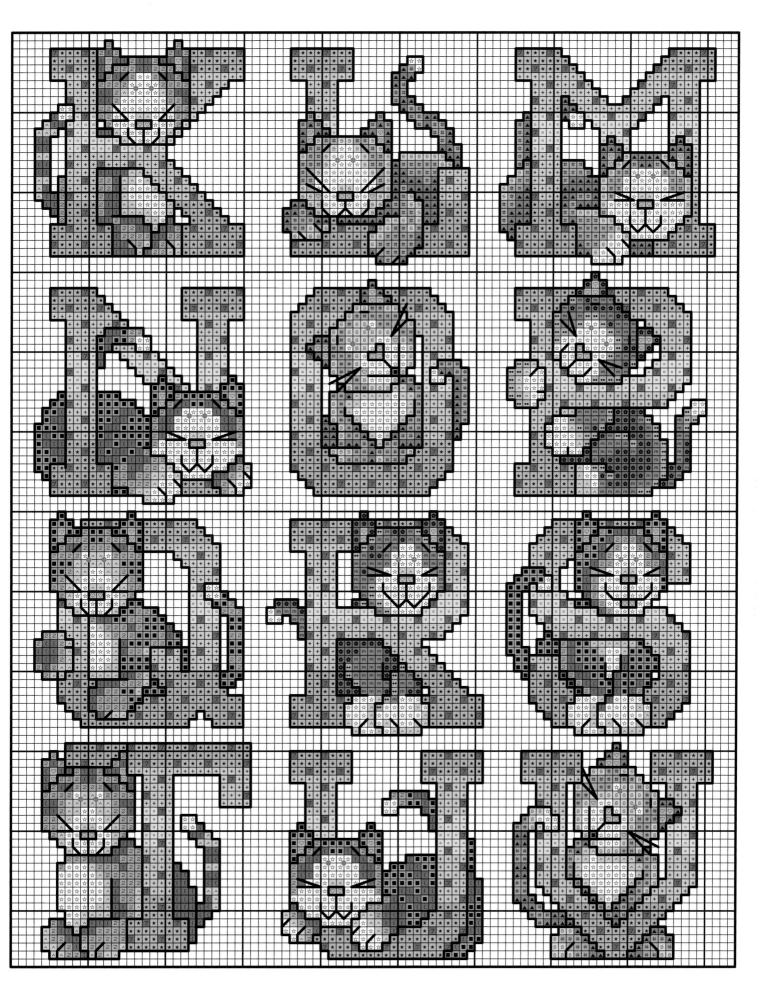

21

KITTIES

X	DMC	B'ST	ANC.	COLOR
☆	blanc		2	white
■	310	╱ *	403	black
(	317		400	dk grey
2	318		399	grey
♥	349		13	red
∧	415		398	lt grey
S	676		891	lt gold
#	729		890	gold
★	742		303	dk yellow
+	743		302	yellow
○	744		301	lt yellow
7	798		131	blue
m	976		1001	brown
◆◆	977		1002	lt brown
♡	3716		25	pink
✿	3826		1049	dk brown
▲	3829		901	dk gold
●	310		403	black Fr. Knot

*Work long stitches for whiskers.

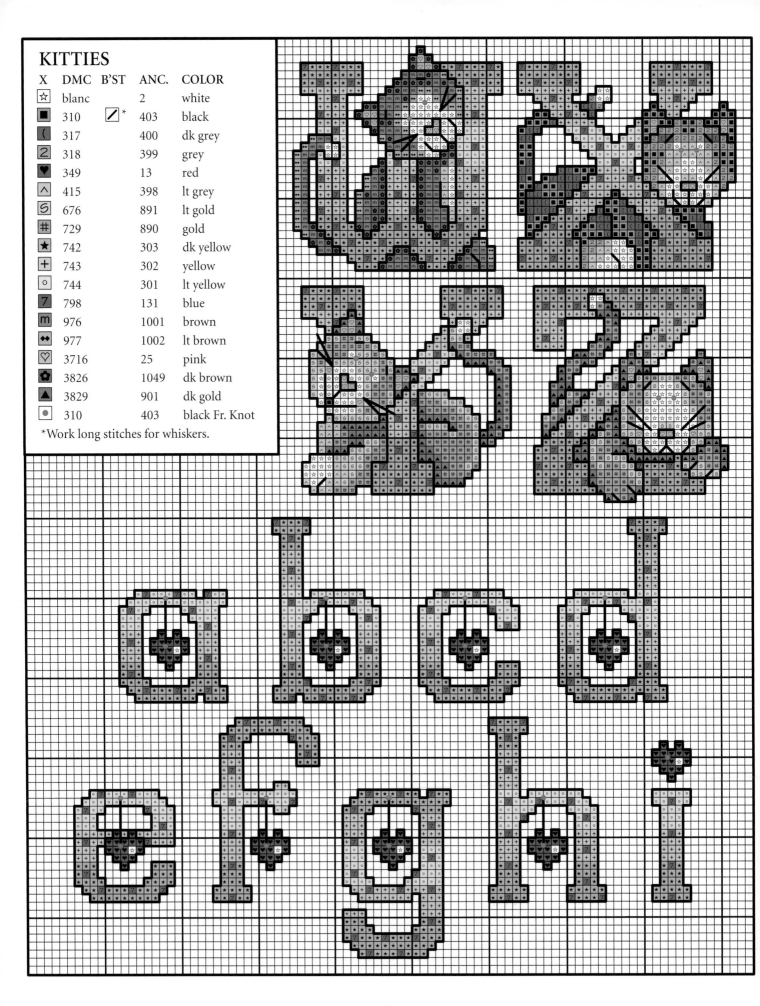

22

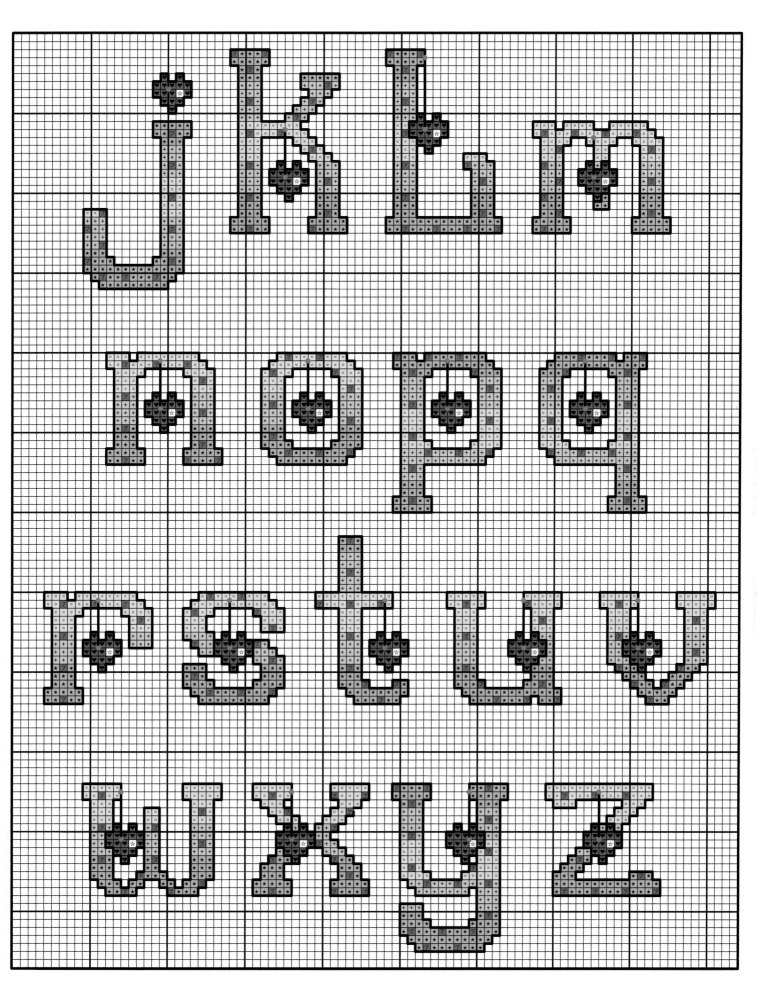

TUMBLING TEDDIES

X	DMC	¼X	B'ST	ANC.	COLOR
☆	blanc			2	white
■	310			403	black
♡	353	◪		6	peach
4	553	◪		98	lavender
	602		／	63	dk pink
+	604	◪		55	pink
∧	676	◪		891	lt gold
○	677	◪		886	vy lt gold
★	680	◪		901	dk gold
#	729	◪		890	gold
↑	743			302	yellow
◇	799	◪		136	blue
6	907	◪		255	green
◼	938		／	381	brown
✳	943	◪		188	turquoise
(	959	◪		186	lt turquoise
–	964	◪		185	vy lt turquoise
	991		／	1076	dk turquoise
●	310			403	black Fr. Knot

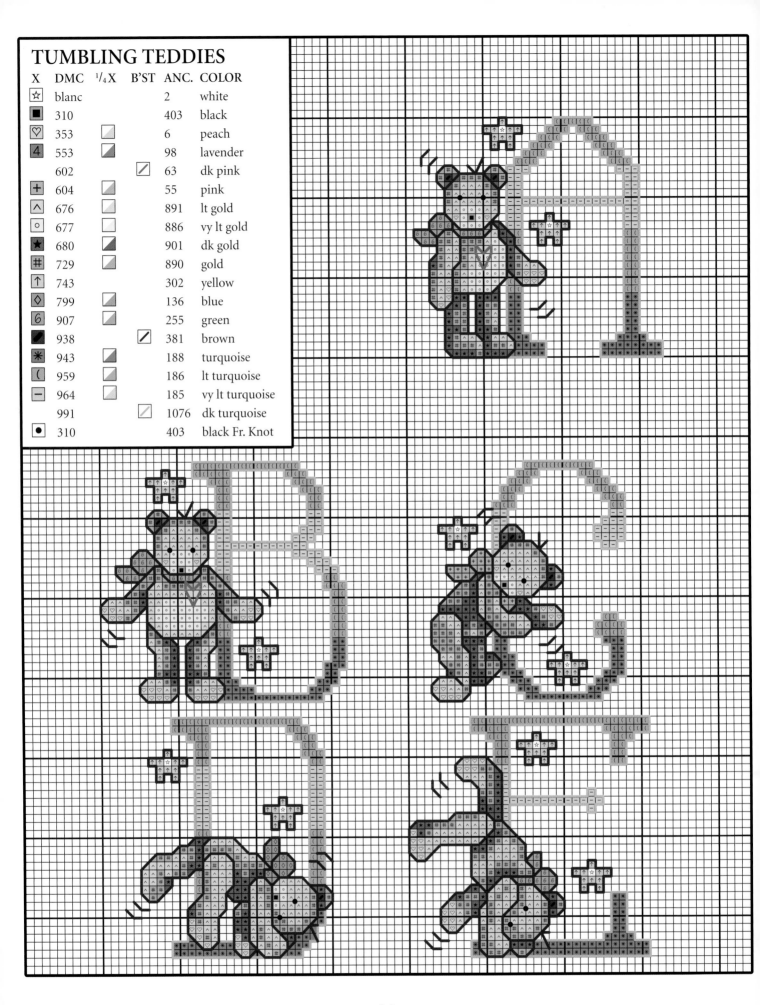

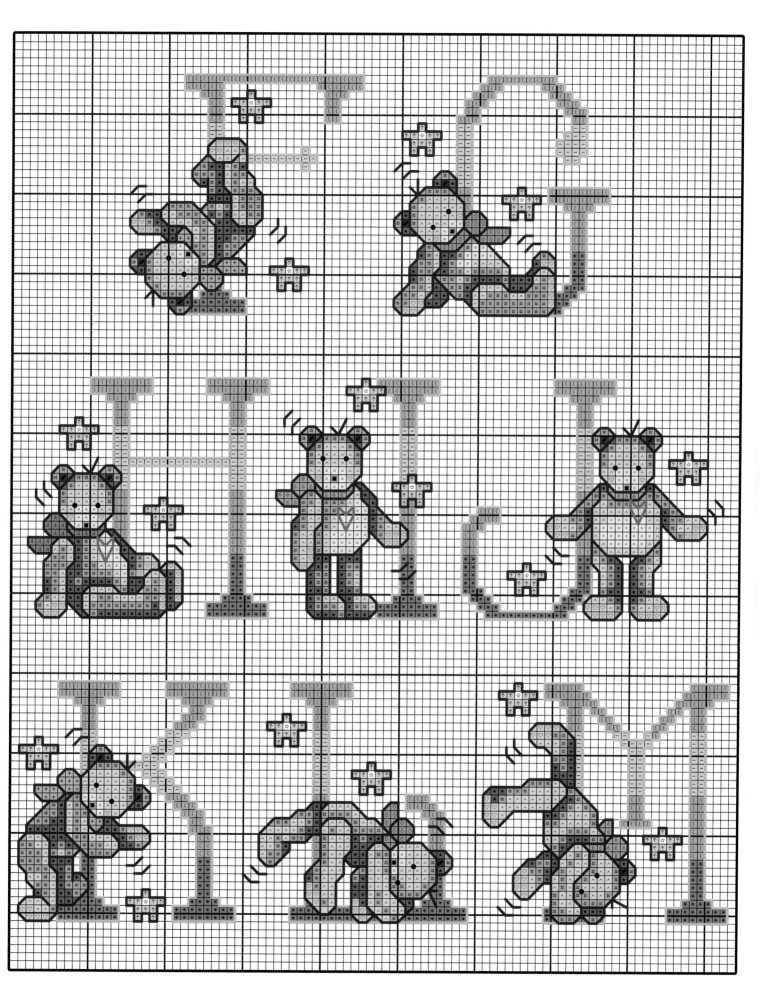

TUMBLING TEDDIES

X	DMC	¼X	B'ST	ANC.	COLOR
☆	blanc			2	white
■	310			403	black
♡	353	◩		6	peach
4	553	◩		98	lavender
	602		╱	63	dk pink
+	604	◩		55	pink
∧	676	◩		891	lt gold
○	677	◩		886	vy lt gold
★	680	◩		901	dk gold
#	729	◩		890	gold
↑	743			302	yellow
◇	799	◩		136	blue
6	907	◩		255	green
◢	938		╱	381	brown
✳	943	◩		188	turquoise
(	959	◩		186	lt turquoise
−	964	◩		185	vy lt turquoise
	991		╱	1076	dk turquoise
●	310			403	black Fr. Knot

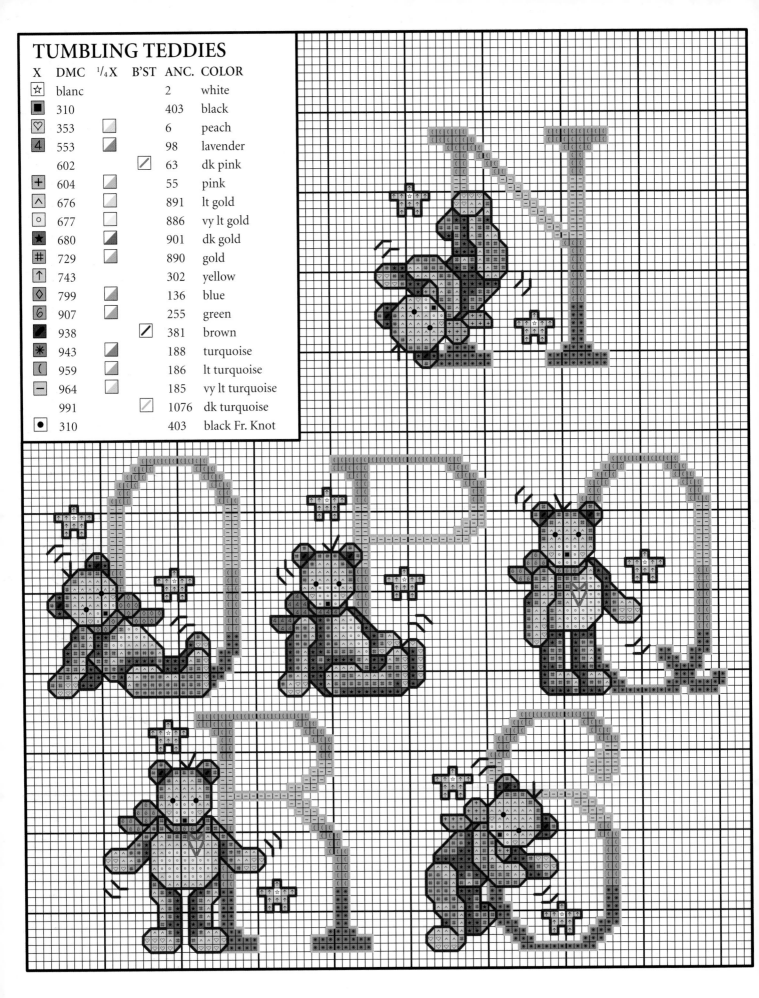

26

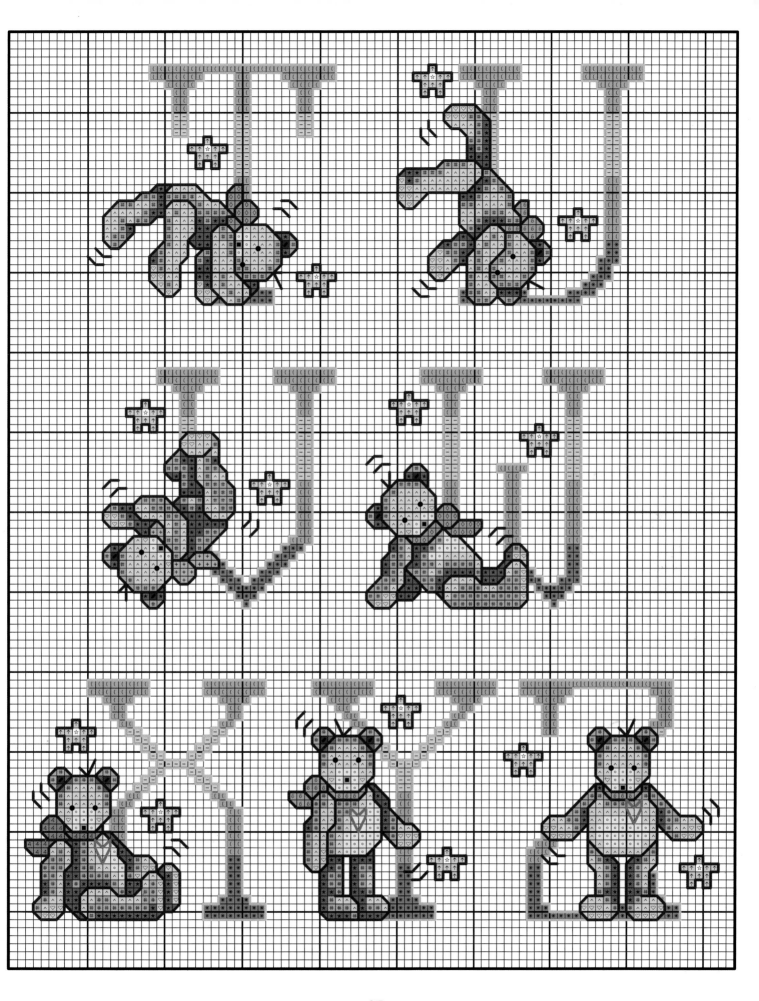

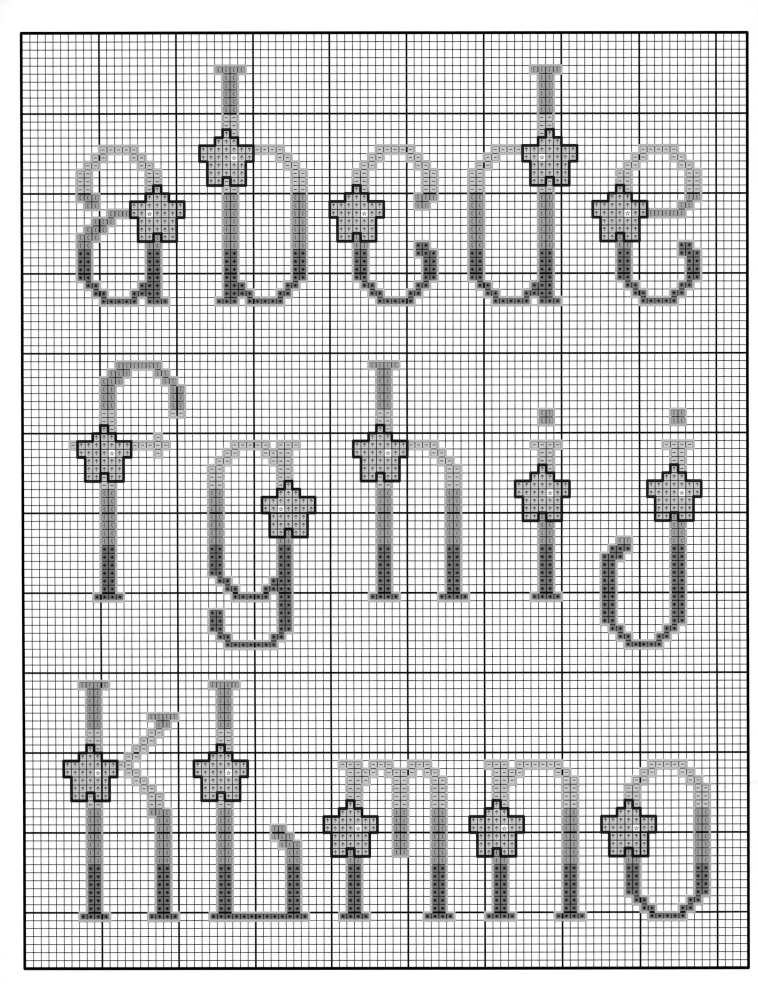

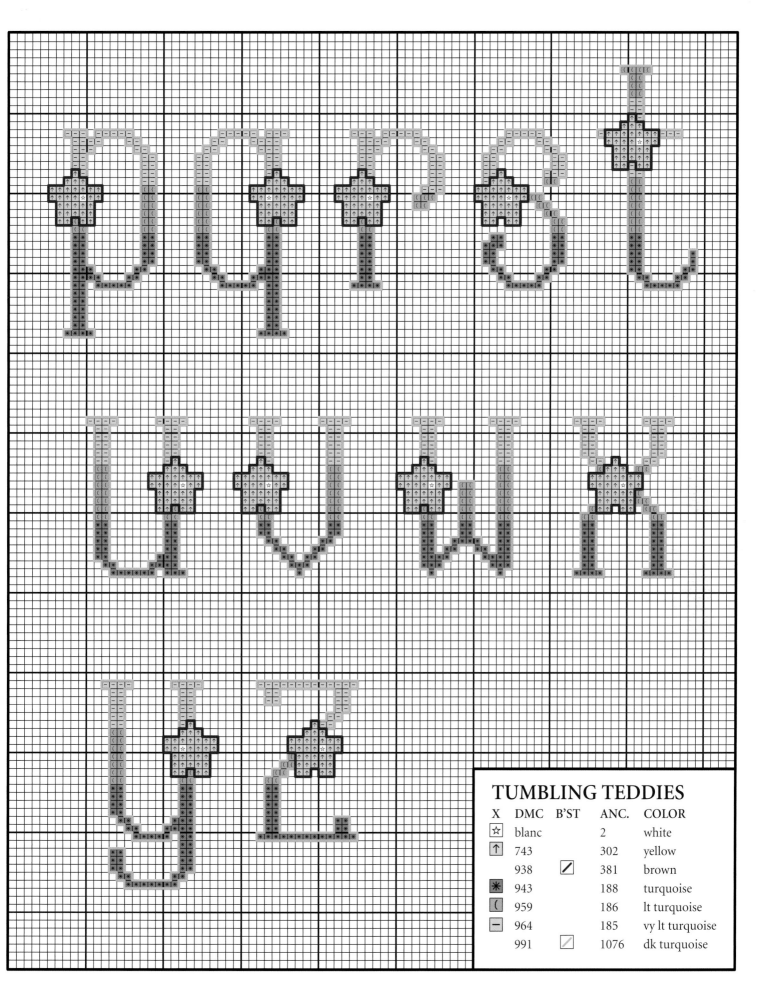

TUMBLING TEDDIES

X	DMC	B'ST	ANC.	COLOR
☆	blanc		2	white
↑	743		302	yellow
	938	╱	381	brown
✳	943		188	turquoise
(	959		186	lt turquoise
−	964		185	vy lt turquoise
	991	╱	1076	dk turquoise

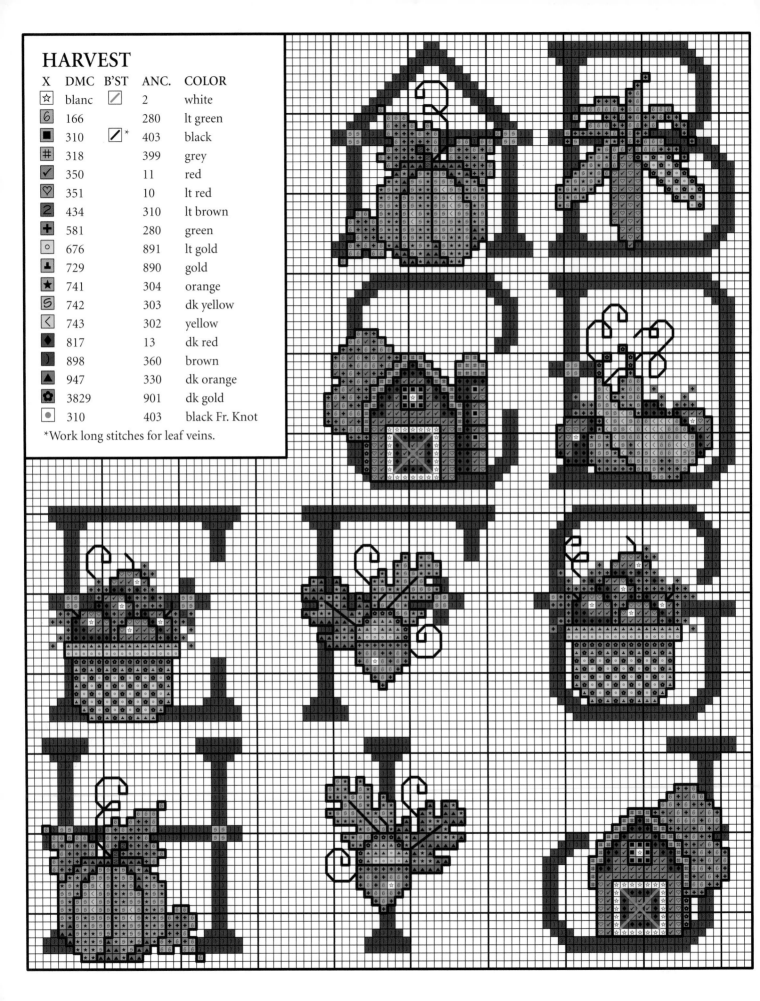

HARVEST

X	DMC	B'ST	ANC.	COLOR
☆	blanc	╱	2	white
6	166		280	lt green
■	310	╱ *	403	black
#	318		399	grey
✓	350		11	red
♡	351		10	lt red
2	434		310	lt brown
✛	581		280	green
○	676		891	lt gold
⬐	729		890	gold
★	741		304	orange
S	742		303	dk yellow
<	743		302	yellow
◆	817		13	dk red
)	898		360	brown
▲	947		330	dk orange
✿	3829		901	dk gold
●	310		403	black Fr. Knot

*Work long stitches for leaf veins.

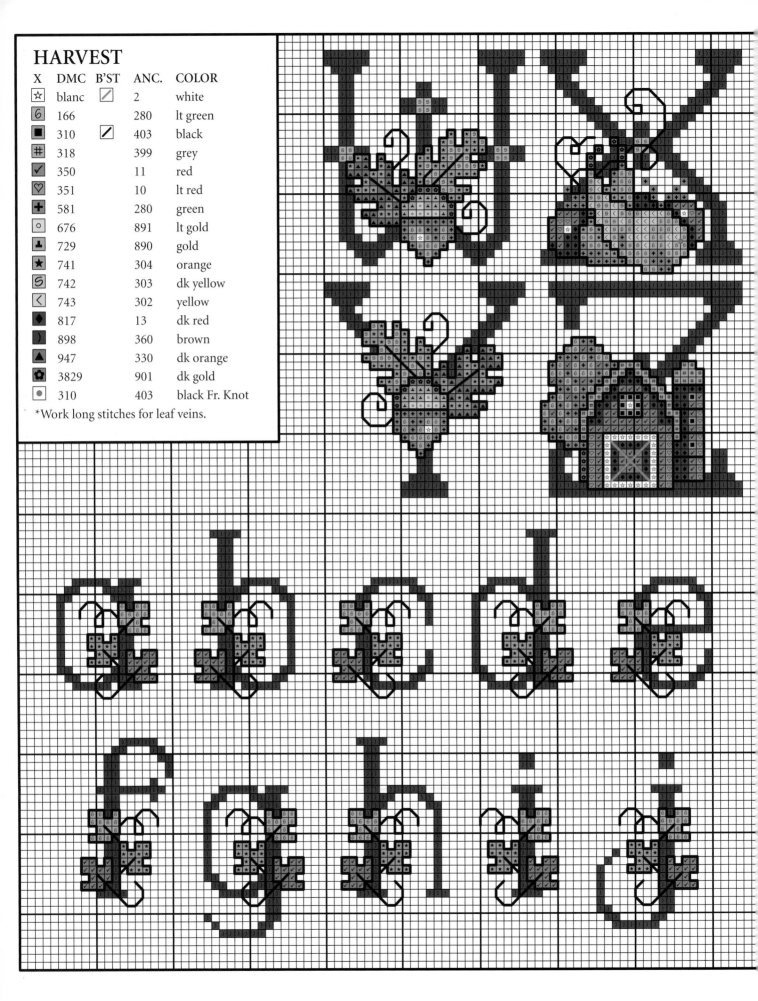

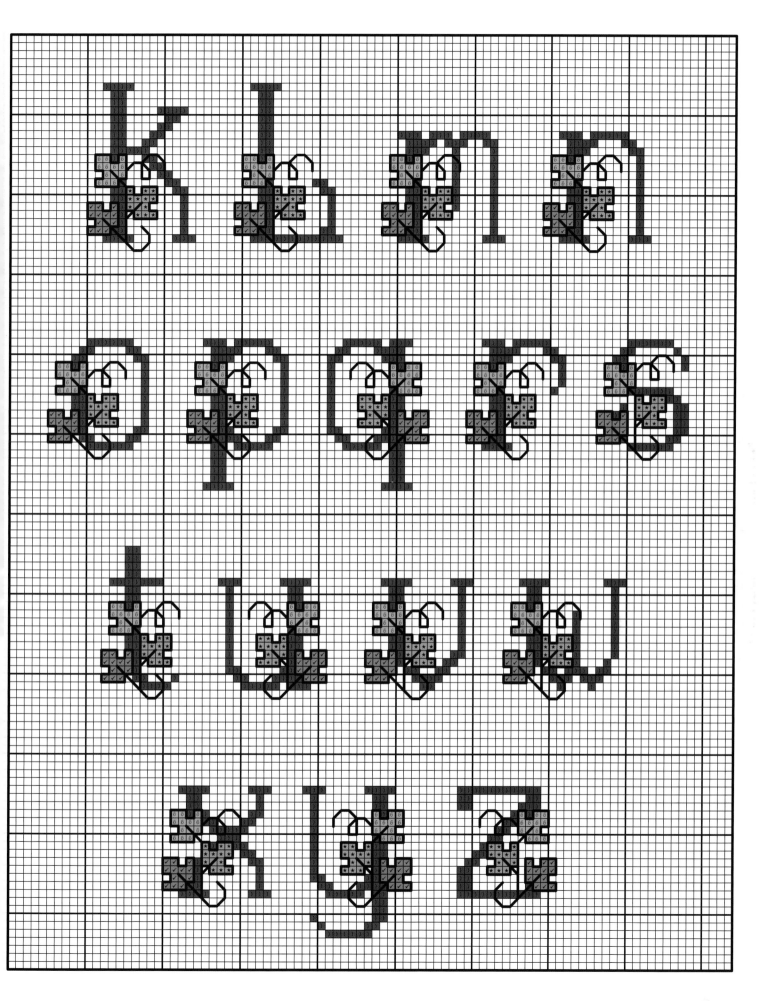

PIRATES

X	DMC	¼X	B'ST	ANC.	COLOR
☆	blanc			2	white
)	208			110	dk lavender
✿	209			109	lavender
^	210			108	lt lavender
■	310		╱*	403	black
✦	350			11	red
✚	351			10	lt red
4	434			310	brown
♡	605			1094	pink
◐	700			228	dk green
✓	729			890	lt brown
★	741			304	orange
▶	798			131	dk blue

X	DMC	¼X	ANC.	COLOR
8	799		136	blue
◆	801		359	dk brown
▼	817		13	dk red
↑	906		256	green
m	907		255	lt green
−	951		1010	peach
✳	972		298	dk yellow
#	973		297	yellow
♣	3325		129	lt blue
●	310		403	black Fr. Knot
•	729		890	lt brown Fr. Knot

*Work long stitches for crossbones on pirates' shirts.

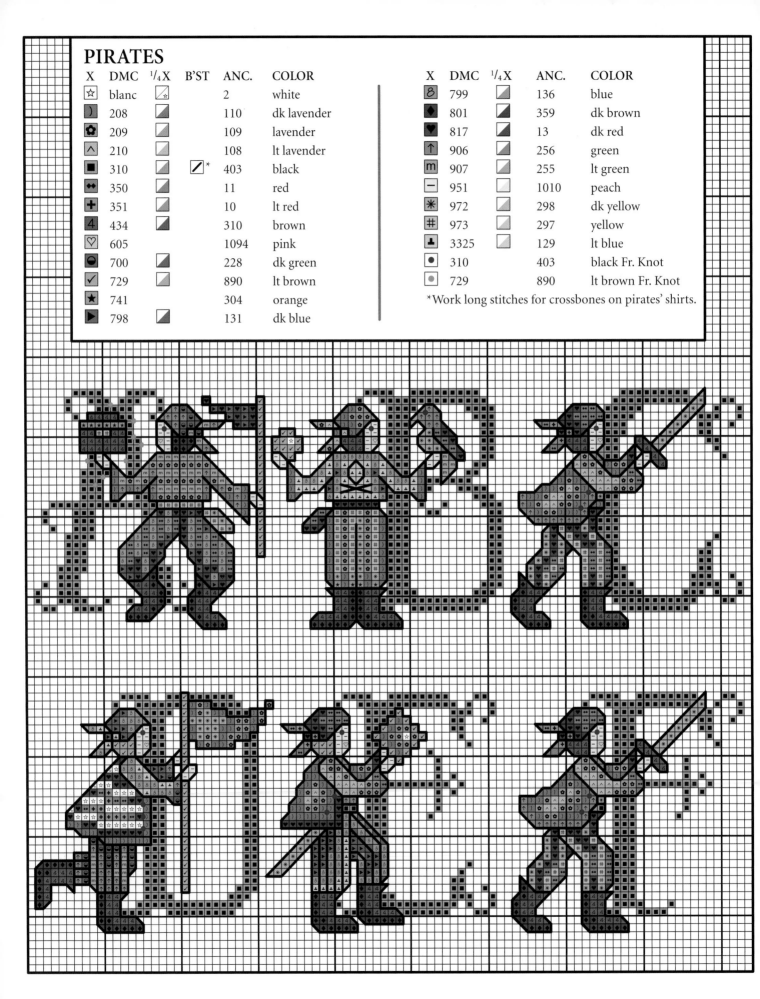

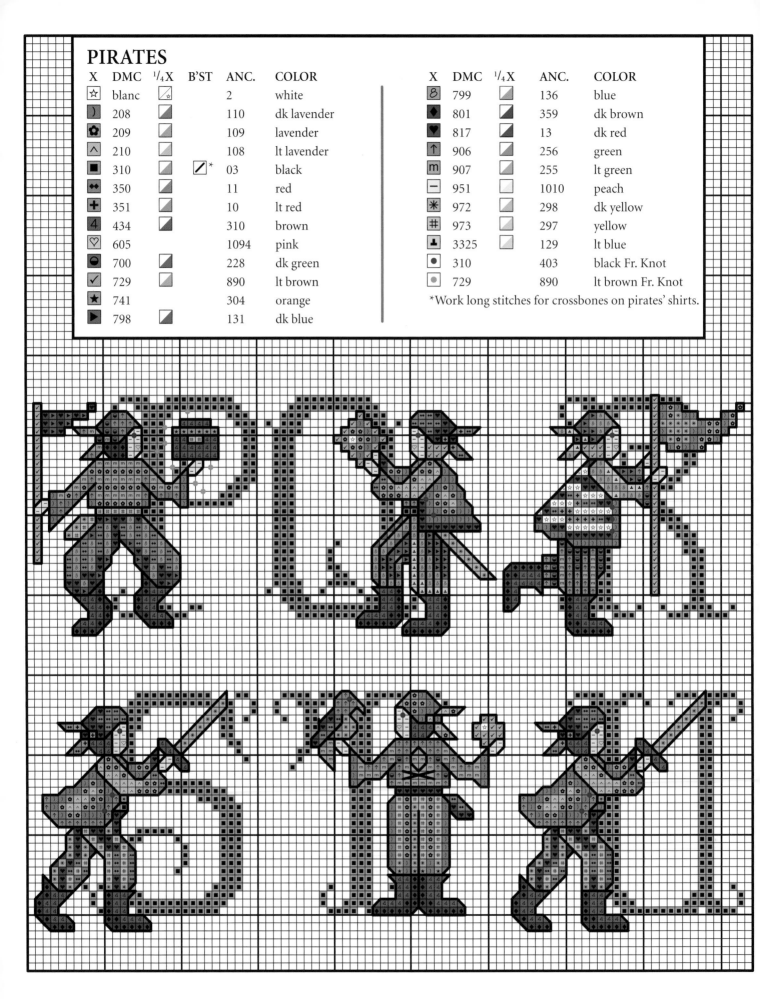

PIRATES

X	DMC	¼X	B'ST	ANC.	COLOR
☆	blanc			2	white
)	208			110	dk lavender
✿	209			109	lavender
∧	210			108	lt lavender
■	310		⁄*	03	black
♦♦	350			11	red
✚	351			10	lt red
4	434			310	brown
♡	605			1094	pink
◖	700			228	dk green
✓	729			890	lt brown
★	741			304	orange
▶	798			131	dk blue
8	799			136	blue
◆	801			359	dk brown
♥	817			13	dk red
↑	906			256	green
m	907			255	lt green
−	951			1010	peach
✳	972			298	dk yellow
#	973			297	yellow
⊥	3325			129	lt blue
●	310			403	black Fr. Knot
⊙	729			890	lt brown Fr. Knot

*Work long stitches for crossbones on pirates' shirts.

36

PIRATES

X	DMC	B'ST	ANC.	COLOR
☆	blanc		2	white
)	208		110	dk lavender
✿	209		109	lavender
■	310	/	403	black
◆◆	350		11	red
◒	700		228	dk green
✓	729		890	lt brown
8	799		136	blue
♥	817		13	dk red
↑	906		256	green
┻	3325		129	lt blue

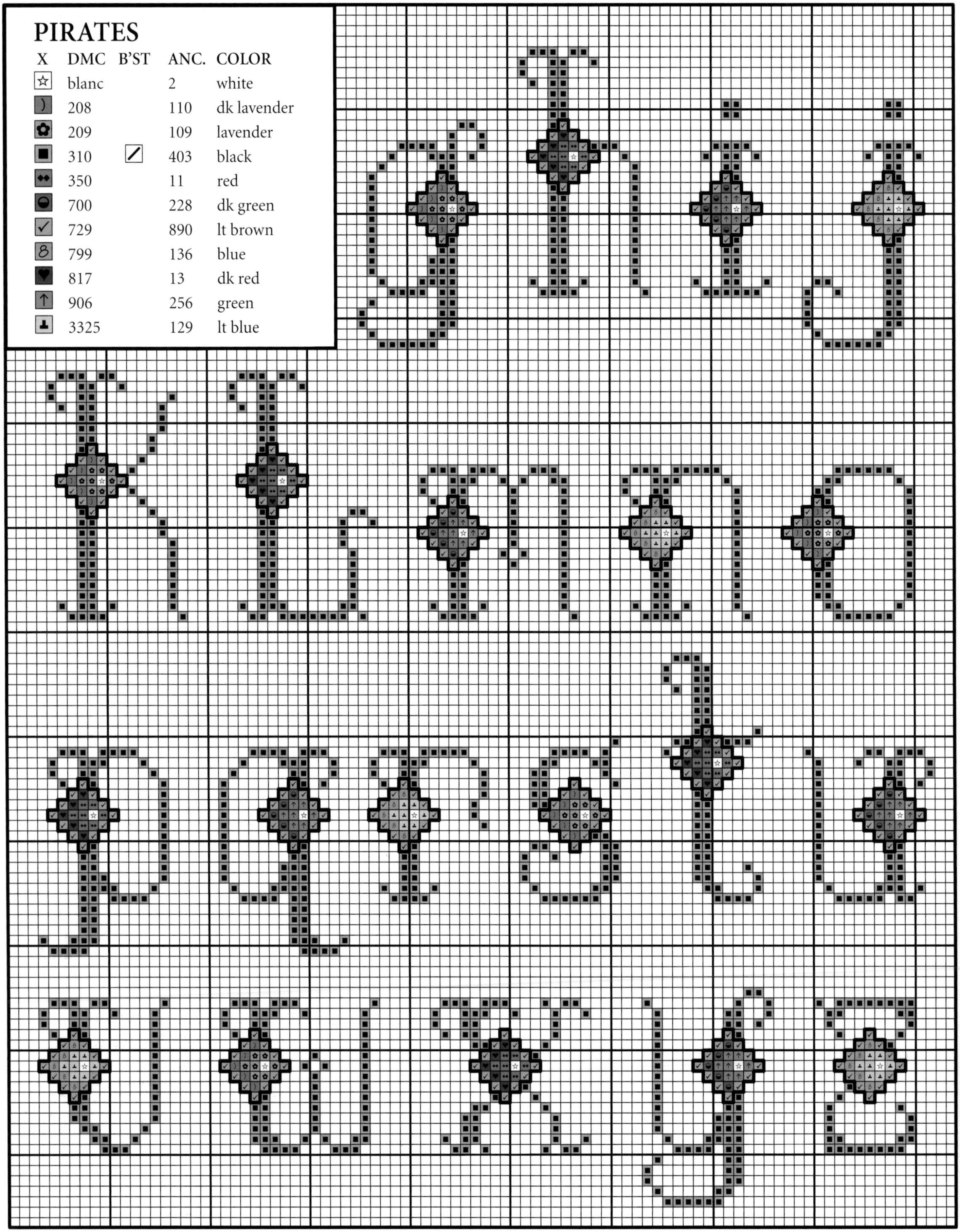

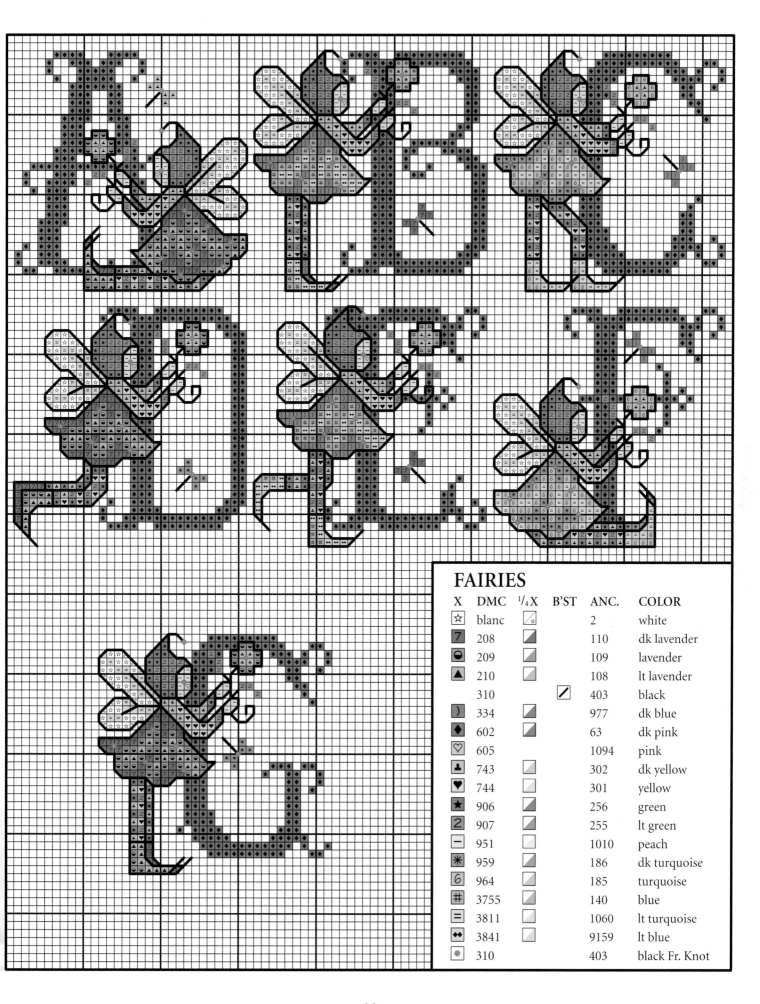

FAIRIES

X	DMC	¼X	B'ST	ANC.	COLOR
☆	blanc	☆		2	white
7	208	◨		110	dk lavender
◖	209	◨		109	lavender
▲	210	◨		108	lt lavender
	310		╱	403	black
)	334	◨		977	dk blue
◆	602	◨		63	dk pink
♡	605	◨		1094	pink
⬓	743	◨		302	dk yellow
♥	744	◨		301	yellow
★	906	◨		256	green
2	907	◨		255	lt green
–	951	◨		1010	peach
✳	959	◨		186	dk turquoise
6	964	◨		185	turquoise
#	3755	◨		140	blue
=	3811	◨		1060	lt turquoise
◆◆	3841	◨		9159	lt blue
●	310			403	black Fr. Knot

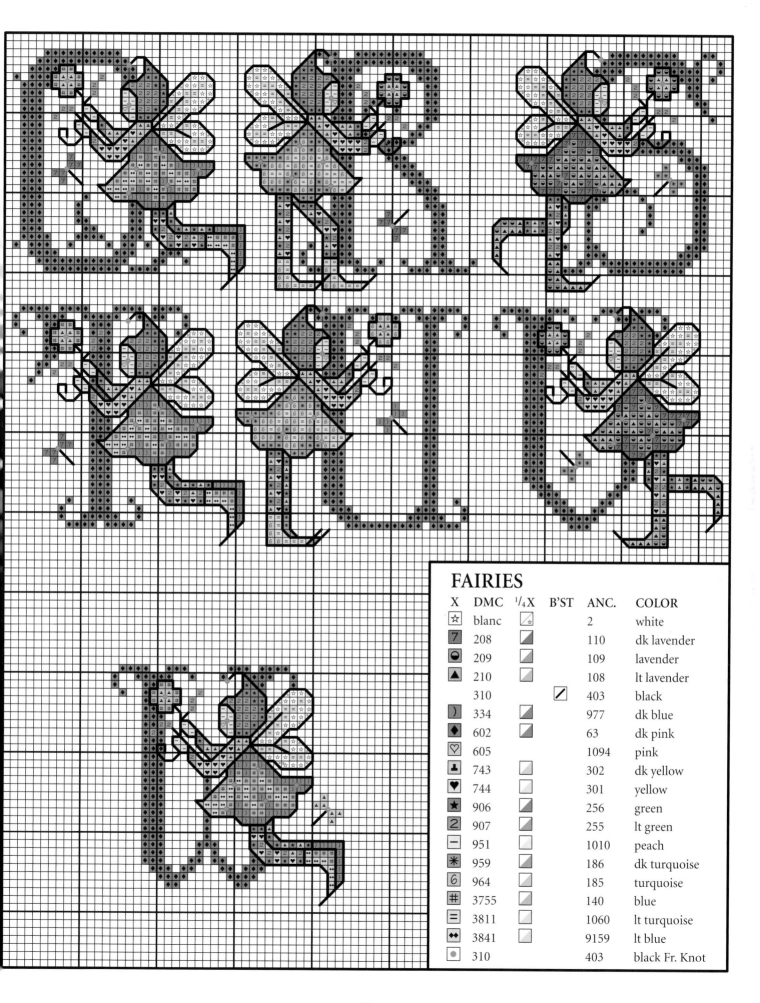

FAIRIES

X	DMC	¼X	B'ST	ANC.	COLOR
☆	blanc	◿		2	white
7	208	◸		110	dk lavender
◖	209	◸		109	lavender
▲	210	◸		108	lt lavender
	310		╱	403	black
)	334	◸		977	dk blue
◆	602	◸		63	dk pink
♡	605			1094	pink
⊥	743	◿		302	dk yellow
♥	744	◿		301	yellow
★	906	◿		256	green
2	907	◸		255	lt green
−	951	◿		1010	peach
✳	959	◸		186	dk turquoise
6	964	◿		185	turquoise
#	3755	◸		140	blue
=	3811	◿		1060	lt turquoise
◆◆	3841	◿		9159	lt blue
●	310			403	black Fr. Knot

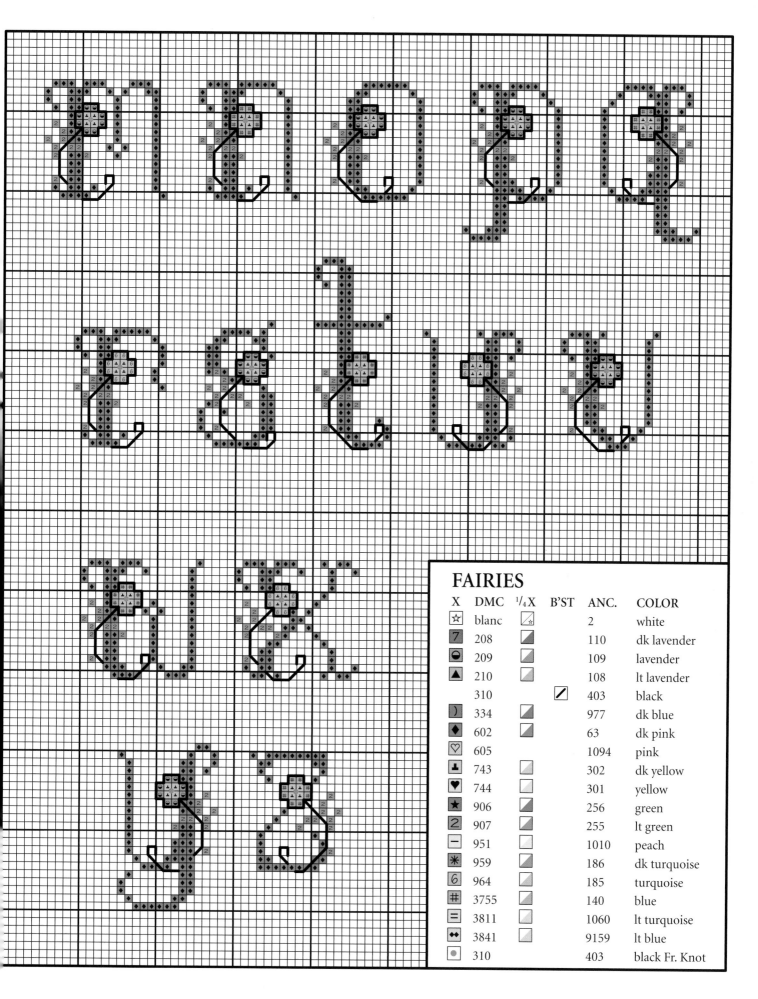

FAIRIES

X	DMC	1/4X	B'ST	ANC.	COLOR
☆	blanc	◹		2	white
7	208	◸		110	dk lavender
◖	209	◸		109	lavender
▲	210	◸		108	lt lavender
	310		╱	403	black
)	334	◸		977	dk blue
◆	602	◸		63	dk pink
♡	605			1094	pink
⊥	743	◹		302	dk yellow
♥	744	◹		301	yellow
★	906	◹		256	green
2	907	◹		255	lt green
─	951	◹		1010	peach
✳	959	◸		186	dk turquoise
6	964	◹		185	turquoise
#	3755	◹		140	blue
═	3811	◹		1060	lt turquoise
◆◆	3841	◹		9159	lt blue
●	310			403	black Fr. Knot

43

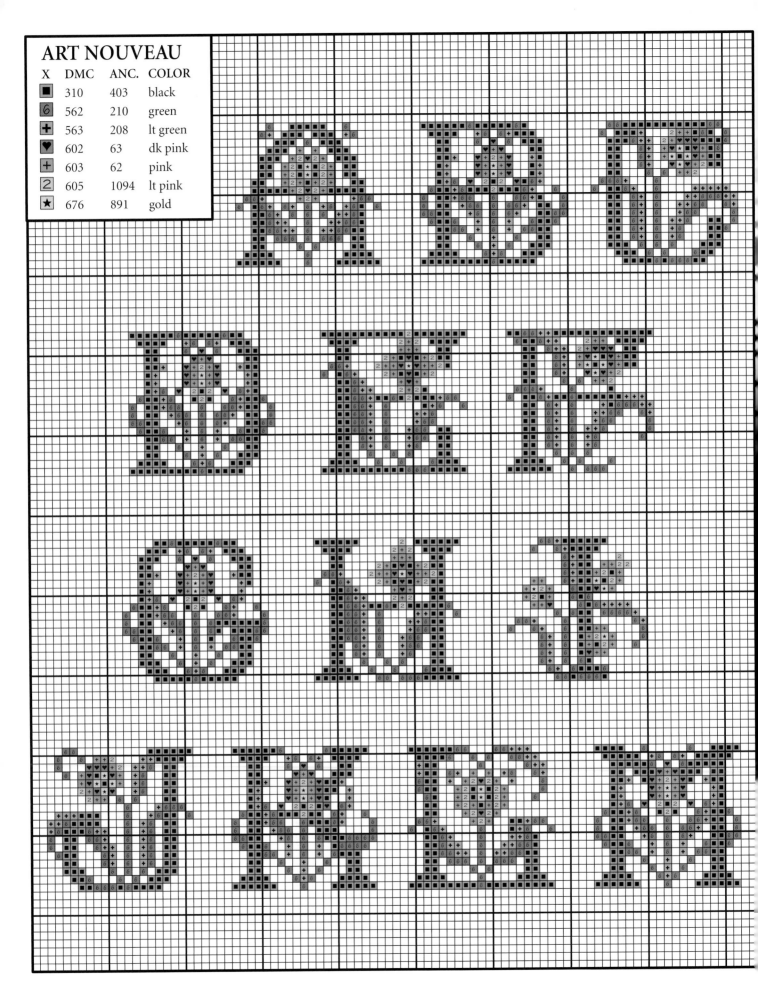

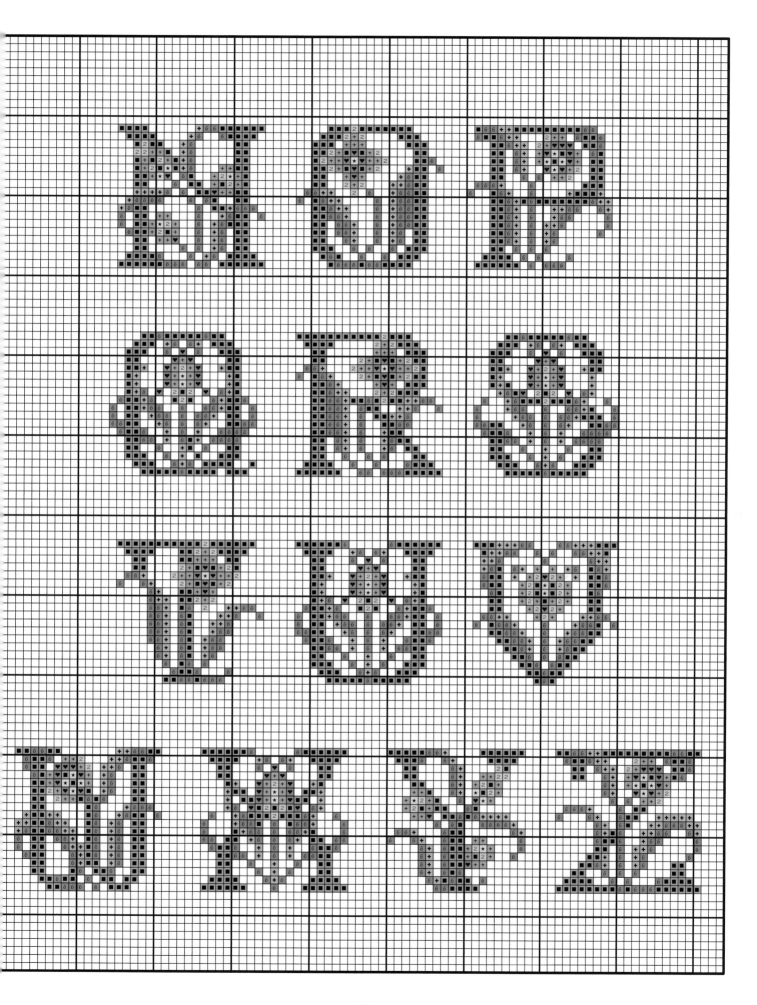

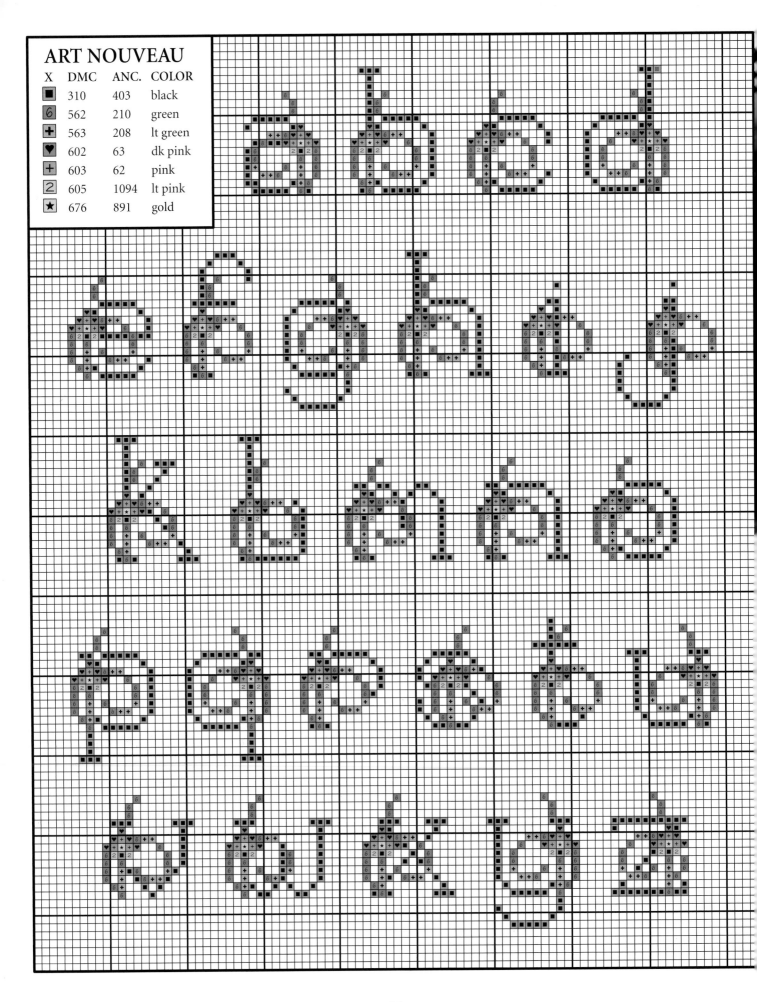

ART NOUVEAU

X	DMC	ANC.	COLOR
■	310	403	black
6	562	210	green
+	563	208	lt green
♥	602	63	dk pink
+	603	62	pink
2	605	1094	lt pink
★	676	891	gold

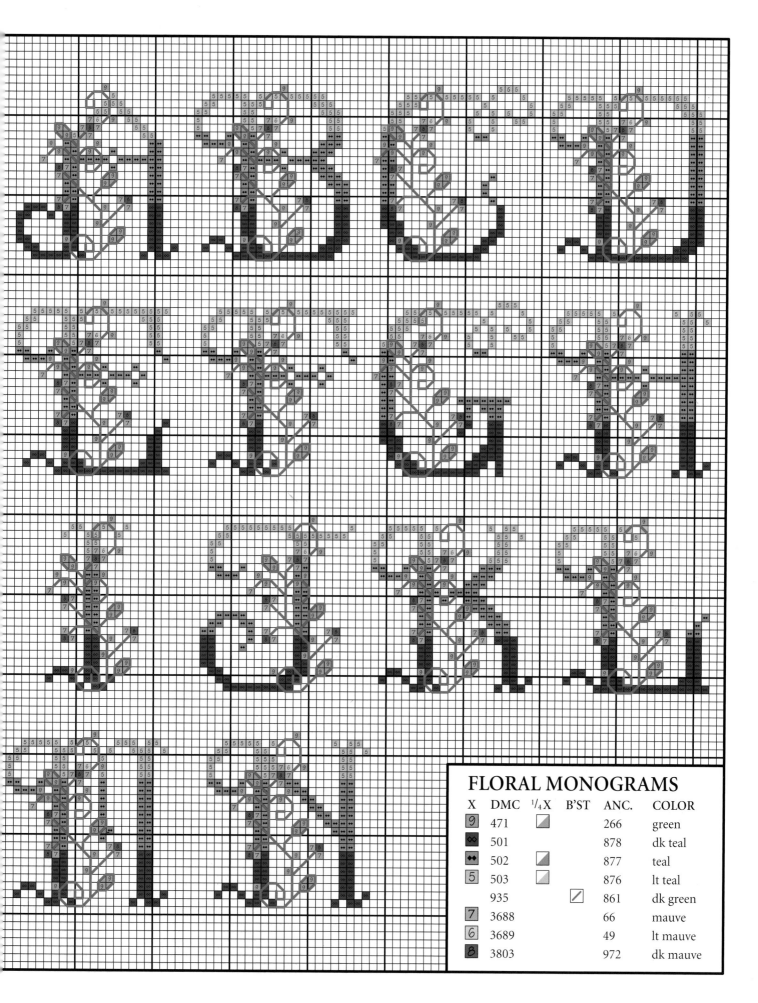

FLORAL MONOGRAMS

X	DMC	¼X	B'ST	ANC.	COLOR
9	471	◩		266	green
✕✕	501			878	dk teal
◆◆	502	◩		877	teal
5	503	◩		876	lt teal
	935		◪	861	dk green
7	3688			66	mauve
6	3689			49	lt mauve
8	3803			972	dk mauve

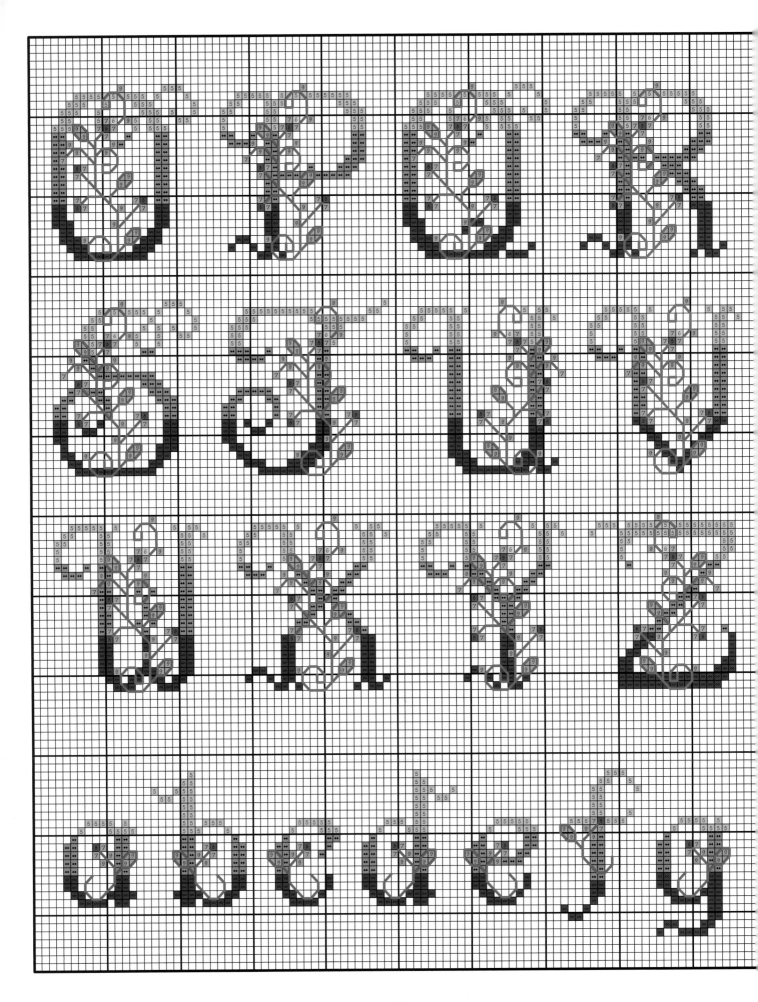

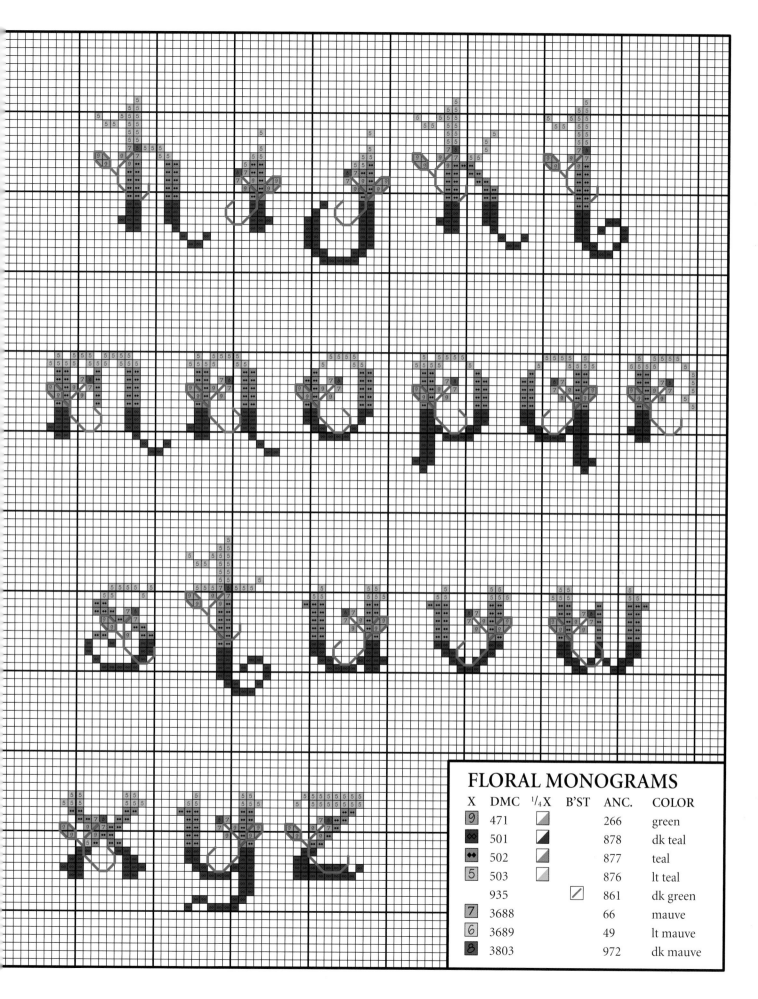

FLORAL MONOGRAMS

X	DMC	¼X	B'ST	ANC.	COLOR
9	471			266	green
✕	501	◢		878	dk teal
◆◆	502	◢		877	teal
5	503	◢		876	lt teal
	935		╱	861	dk green
7	3688			66	mauve
6	3689			49	lt mauve
8	3803			972	dk mauve

GENERAL INSTRUCTIONS

WORKING WITH ALPHABETS
Choosing Your Design
Working with alphabets is all about creativity. You can choose what you want to say and then choose how it looks! Here are some guidelines to help in the creative process.

- **What you plan to stitch on will determine how you design your project.** If you are going to stitch a design on fabric that will be framed or finished in a way where the final size is not crucial, you can use any alphabet you wish and make the design any size you want. If you're going to stitch on a prefinished item, such as a towel or baby bib, then the stitching area on your item may determine the alphabets available for use.
- **Mixing upper case letters with the lower case letters in an alphabet may make a more appealing design.** For example, stitch the first letter of a name with the upper case letter and the rest of the name with the lower case letters.

CHARTING YOUR DESIGN
A Word about Spacing
Spacing between letters and words depends on the alphabet you're using and personal preference. A good starting point is to try leaving one space between letters and three or four spaces between words. If that arrangement looks too spacey or too cramped, alter the spacing until you like the look of your design. Remember, equal spacing is not always the best spacing.

Don't forget that ascending letters like **b**, **d**, **k**, and **l** and descending letters like **g**, **j**, and **p** may take a little more room between rows.

Arranging Your Design
1. Draw the outline of the letters from the chart on graph paper, leaving several spaces between the letters. You may photocopy the graph paper on page 52.
2. Cut the letters apart; arrange the letters on another piece of graph paper until the spacing is appealing.
3. Tape the letters in place.

Fitting a Design to a Specific Stitching Area
If you are planning a design for a prefinished item, you need to make sure your design will fit.

1. Count the stitches in the width and height of your item's stitching area.
2. Draw the stitching area on a piece of graph paper.
3. Chart your letters and arrange them inside the lines following the previous instructions.

STITCHING YOUR DESIGN
Figuring the Size to Cut Your Fabric
1. Count the squares in the width of your design.
2. Divide that number by the thread count of your fabric. This gives you the width of your design in inches when stitched on that particular count fabric.

Examples
63 squares wide ÷ 14 count Aida = $4\frac{1}{2}$" wide
63 squares wide ÷ 18 count Aida = $3\frac{1}{2}$" wide

3. Repeat the process to determine the height of the design.
4. When cutting the fabric, add at least 3" to each side of the design.

Using the Right Number of Floss Strands
The table below gives the recommended number of floss strands for common fabric thread counts.

Thread Count per Inch	Number of Strands for Cross Stitch	Number of Strands for Backstitch	Number of Strands for French Knot
8.5	6	2	4
10 or 11	4 or 5	2	3
12 or 13	3	1	2
14	2 or 3	1	1 or 2
16	2	1	1
18	2	1	1
22	1	1	1

HOW TO READ CHARTS

Each chart is made up of a key and a gridded design where each square represents a stitch. The symbols in the key tell which floss color to use for each stitch in the chart. The following headings and symbols are given:

X – Cross Stitch
DMC – DMC color number
¼X – Quarter Stitch
B'ST – Backstitch
ANC. – Anchor color number
COLOR – The name given to the floss color in this chart

 A square filled with a color and a symbol should be worked as a **Cross Stitch**.

 A triangle should be worked as a **Quarter Stitch**.

 A straight line should be worked as a **Backstitch**.

 A large dot listed near the end of the key should be worked as a **French Knot**.

In the chart, the symbol for a **Cross Stitch** may be omitted or partially covered when a **Backstitch** crosses its square. Refer to the background color to determine the floss color.

HOW TO STITCH

Always work **Cross Stitches** and **Quarter Stitches** first and then add the **Backstitch** and **French Knots**. When stitching, bring the threaded needle up at **1** and all **odd** numbers and down at **2** and all **even** numbers (**Figs. 1–5**).

Cross Stitch (X): For horizontal rows, work stitches in two journeys (**Fig. 1**). For vertical rows, complete each stitch as shown (**Fig. 2**).

Fig. 1   **Fig. 2**

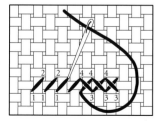   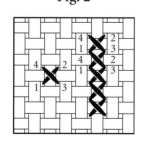

Quarter Stitch (¼X): Come up at **1**, then split the fabric to go down at **2** (**Fig. 3**).

Fig. 3

Backstitch (B'ST): For outlines and details, Backstitch should be worked after the design has been completed (**Fig. 4**).

Fig. 4

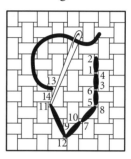

French Knot: Bring the needle up at **1**. Wrap the floss once around the needle. Insert the needle at **2**, tighten the knot, and pull the needle through the fabric, holding the floss until it must be released (**Fig. 5**). For a larger knot, use more floss strands; wrap only once.

Fig. 5

Production Team: Writer – Frances Huddleston; Editorial Writer – Susan Johnson; Senior Graphic Artist – Lora Puls; Graphic Artists – Jacob Casleton and Janie Wright; Photographer – Ken West.

Instructions tested and photography models made by Donna L. Overman, Angie Perryman, and Anne Simpson.

Fabric provided courtesy of Charles Craft, Inc.
Embroidery floss provided courtesy of the DMC Corporation.

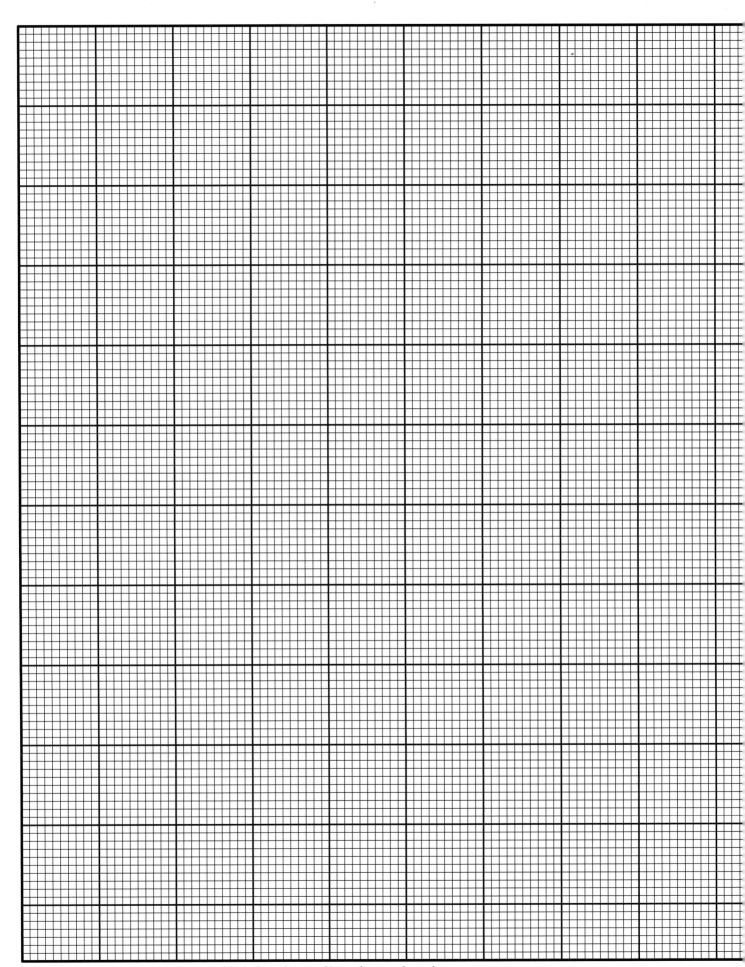